HE IS MY HEAVEN
The Life of
Elizabeth of the Trinity

Jennifer Moorcroft

ICS Publications
Institute of Carmelite Studies
Washington, D.C.

ICS Publications
2131 Lincoln Road, N.E.
Washington, DC 20002-1199
www.icspublications.org

Photos used with permission of the Carmel of Dijon (Dijon-Flavignerot)

Cover design by SayYes Design

Typeset and produced in the United States of America

Library of Congress Cataloging-in-Publication Data

Moorcroft, Jennifer.
He is my heaven: the life of Elizabeth of the Trinity / Jennifer
Moorcroft.
    p. cm.
Includes bibliographical references.
    ISBN: 978-0-935216-25-7 (pbk. : alk. paper)
    1. Elizabeth of the Trinity, Sister, 1880–1906. 2. Christian saints—
France—Biography. 3. Carmelite Nuns—France—Biography. 4.
Mystics—France—Biography. I. Title
BX4700.E44 M66 2001
271'.97102—dc21   00-057568

CONTENTS

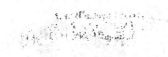

HE IS MY HEAVEN

The Life of
Elizabeth of the Trinity

Elizabeth Catez
A formal photograph at age 20. It was taken in June 1901,
two months before she entered the Dijon Carmel.

AUTHOR'S INTRODUCTION

To write the biography of a saint is a special experience. You have to put her in her historical context, recount her doings, try to enter into her thoughts and feelings, and plot her life from birth to death. But death is not the end of the story; the saint is alive beyond all our imaginings. She is now eternally a member of the family of God and, however unequal the relationship, becomes a familiar friend and companion on the way.

I first "met" Elizabeth of the Trinity some forty years ago when I read *The Praise of Glory,* her biography written by her prioress, and the fascination and love of her writings have endured.

There is a discussion going on at present in Prague as to whether some form of monument—a street named after him, perhaps—should be dedicated to its most famous son, the author Franz Kafka. Both sides agree that he himself would want no such thing, since he was a very retiring man, who shunned the limelight. It is the glorious paradox of Christianity that a saint would not mind at all being known and written about because, in describing the lives of saints, we are praising not what they have achieved by their own efforts but the triumph of grace in each person and what God has done in and through them. The biography of a saint is, as it were, a biography of the Holy Spirit at work at this particular time, in this particular person.

In the case of Elizabeth of the Trinity, it is also an attempt to make her teachings on the spiritual life better known and appreciated. The media can hardly mention the church without bemoaning—or perhaps gloating—on its dwindling numbers, especially in Britain. People are no less interested in the search for meaning and some form of spirituality than they ever were, but increasingly they seem to search for it everywhere but in Christianity. And yet, when it is manifested in so attractive a manner as in the life of Elizabeth of the Trinity, it must surely draw people first to desire it and then to attempt to follow, even if it is in a far feebler manner than that shown by Elizabeth herself. Christianity is often caricatured as joyless and repressive;

Elizabeth, by her sheer happiness in the life she was called to, shows that those who are living in the love of God are the truly happy ones, even when, as in Elizabeth's case, this was in the midst of severe suffering.

Elizabeth longed for her teaching to be known and put into practice. Toward the end of her life she wrote that "It seems to me that in heaven my mission will be to draw people and help them to go out of themselves to adhere to God by a very simple and loving way, and to keep them in that great inner silence that will allow God to be imprinted within them, to transform them into himself."

Her mission was to inspire people to pray, and her teaching is not confined to those in the cloister. Our world is far more cluttered, noisy, and distracting than hers ever was, but the message is still valid. With quiet and persistent perseverance, we can acquire the habit of going into that quiet place within ourselves where he is, and to live in his presence there, wherever we are.

There are many techniques of prayer, but for a Christian it is vital to know to whom your prayer is directed. For Elizabeth, it was her "Three," the Triune God—Father, Son, and Spirit—fully revealed by Jesus, the Son of God. Pope John Paul II designated the three years leading up to the millennium to the three Persons, and as we celebrate the new millennium of the coming of Jesus Christ into his world, the life and writings of Elizabeth of the Trinity are particularly apt. As the *Catechism of the Catholic Church* states, "The mystery of the Most Holy Trinity is the central mystery of Christian faith and life. It is the mystery of God in himself" (*Catechism*, 234). The *Catechism* also says that "The ultimate end of the whole divine economy is the entry of God's creatures into the perfect unity of the Blessed Trinity. But even now we are called to be a dwelling for the Most Holy Trinity" (*Catechism*, 260). It is no accident that the *Catechism* concludes this section with Elizabeth's famous prayer. Her life and teaching is a commentary on this passage of the *Catechism*.

Many writers on Elizabeth comment on the narrow range of her spirituality, compared, for example, with St. Thérèse of Lisieux, her contemporary. Elizabeth could perhaps be compared to a magnifying glass. By concentrating the rays of the sun, a magnifying glass can set wood ablaze; at the same time, it expands the vision. The very intensity of Elizabeth's focus on prayer and union with God in love is meant as a message to us, to remind us that union with God is the calling of every human being. It is what we were created for, and prayer should be the very air we breathe as we live out our calling.

If the range of Elizabeth's teaching is narrow, the expansiveness of her love is not. Because her gaze is fixed unswervingly on nothing less than God, her horizon, as she said, is infinite. With her family she traveled widely in France and Switzerland, and the majestic scenery moved her deeply. She loved, too, the vast expanses of the ocean, because they reminded her of the infinity of God. She could only bear to leave it all behind because the vistas opened up to her in Carmel were so much greater. This sense of the grandeur, the greatness, and the majesty of God, who has at the same time drawn so close to us as to be with us at every moment of every day in his total love for us, is a timely message that Elizabeth expresses so beautifully.

In writing this biography I have drawn heavily on the *Complete Works* of Elizabeth's writings and, in particular, the invaluable footnotes. In describing Elizabeth's thoughts and feelings, I have drawn solely on what she herself expressed in her writings and on the testimonies of those close to her.

I wish to express my thanks to my husband David for his encouragement and support while writing this book. It was with great relief I could turn to his linguistic skills to back up my schoolgirl French. And I owe the Carmelite sisters of Ware a debt of gratitude I can never repay fully, although I hope this book will go some way as a tribute to all they taught me of the Carmelite way of life.

ABBREVIATIONS AND CITATIONS

In this biography, the following abbreviations are used followed by the page number, except where indicated by paragraph number (+ par. no.) or piece number (e.g., letters, poems, and notes). An asterisk (*) indicates where the author has provided her original English translation from the French edition.

AP	"Procès Apostolique" in *Summarium* of the cause of beatification of Elizabeth.
CE	"Composition Exercises" of Elizabeth of the Trinity in PAT.
D	Diary—"Journal" (+ par. no.) in JTD, v. II.*
EP	"Enquête Philipon" in PAT*
GV	"The Greatness of Our Vocation" (+ par. no.) in Works, v. 1.
HF	"Heaven in Faith" (+ par. no.) in Works, v. 1.
JTD	*J'ai Trouvé Dieu: Oeuvres Complètes* (3 vols), Paris: Editions du Cerf, 1980, 1980, 1979.*
L	Letter— "The Early Letters" (#1–83) in JTD, v. II*; "The Letters from Carmel" (#84–342) in Works, v. 2.
LLL	*Light Love Life,* ed. by Conrad De Meester et al., Washington, DC: ICS Publications, 1987, 1995, 2012.
LR	"Last Retreat" (+ par. no.) in Works, v. 1.
LYL	"Let Yourself Be Loved" (+ par. no.) in Works, v. 1.
NI	"Notes Intimes" (#1–17) in JTD, v. II.*
P	"Poem" (#1–123) in JTD, v. II.*

PAT   *Elisabeth de la Trinité: Paroles, annotations person-nelles et premiers témoins oculaires*

PG   *The Praise of Glory,* ed. by the Benedictines of Stanbrook Abbey, London: Burns Oates & Washbourne, 1913.

RB   "Récit biographique" (biographical account) in PAT.

SD   *The Spiritual Doctrine of Elizabeth of the Trinity,* by M.M. Philipon, Washington, DC: Teresian Charism Press, 1985.

SOS   *Story of a Soul,* ed. by John Clarke, Washington, DC: ICS Publications, 1975, 3rd edition 1996.

Souv.   *Souvenirs,* ed. by the Carmel of Dijon, Paris: Editions St. Paul, 1945.

Works   *The Complete Works of Elizabeth of the Trinity* (2 vols), Washington, DC: ICS Publications, 1984, 1995, 2014.

PART ONE
The Early Years

1

A REAL LITTLE DEVIL
Early Childhood

Elizabeth Catez, whose imagination would be enthralled by the sight of charging cavalry, polished helmets, and cuirasses glinting in the sun, was born into a military family.

Her mother, Marie Rolland, was born in Lunéville on August 30, 1846, the only daughter of Commandant Raymond Rolland of the seventh Regiment of Hussars and Josephine Klein of Lunéville. Elizabeth's father, on the other hand, came from a less distinguished background and made his way up the ranks the hard way. Joseph Catez was born in Aire-sur-la-Lys on May 29, 1832, the fourth of seven children of André Cattez and Fideline Hoel. His father was a farm hand who never learned to read and write; he died when Joseph was eight years old. His mother died in 1876, so as Elizabeth grew up, it was her mother's family with whom she had most contact.

Joseph had no wish to work on the farm, so at the age of twenty-one he dropped a "t" from his name and enlisted as a volunteer with the eighth Squadron of the Equipment and Maintenance Corps. He was in the Algerian campaign for almost nine years and was later taken prisoner in Sedan during the War of 1870. He was promoted to lieutenant in 1872 and made captain in 1875.

Shortly afterward he was posted to Lunel (Hérault) where he met Marie Rolland. On September 3, 1879, they were married. Neither of them was young—Joseph was forty-seven; Marie, thirty-three. In many ways their characters were very disparate. Joseph had an outgoing and good-natured love of life; he loved his beer and his cigars and being with his fellow soldiers. Marie had a much more strong-willed character, tending to the Jansenistic. Before she met Joseph, she had at one time been engaged to be married, but her fiancé had been killed in the War of 1870, which gave her an added seriousness. However, the one thing they had in common was a deep faith, and it was this faith that bound them together and made their marriage strong and rich. It gave Joseph's character an integrity and nobility that won him not only the liking but also the respect and esteem of his fellow officers and men. And Marie's strength of will was to carry her through some difficult times ahead.

For the present, though, there was much to look forward to. Joseph was posted at the army camp in Avor, the first of many new postings in their married life, and something they both became used to. And Marie discovered she was pregnant.

It proved to be a difficult birth. Marie went into a long and difficult labor that lasted thirty-six hours. In the early hours of the morning on July 18, 1880, Joseph was warned that they might lose the baby. He immediately hurried up the tree-lined avenue toward the chapel, where the chaplain, Captain Chaboisseau, was preparing to say Mass, to ask him to offer the Mass for the safety of his wife and child. Just as the Mass was ending, Elizabeth was born, healthy, "a very beautiful, very lively child" (RB 1:1; LLL 25), as Mme. Catez was later to write proudly.

The day was a Sunday, something that pleased Elizabeth greatly in later years, as did the date of her baptism a few days later on July 22, the feast of St. Mary Magdalene, the one "who loved much."

The army camp of Avor was "a quite rustic barracks which I'd have been happy to live in" (CE 22; LLL 24), as Elizabeth was to write. In those country surroundings Mme. Catez was able to regain her strength after the stress of Elizabeth's birth. She had a maid, Héloïse, to help her, and she soon began to write glowing letters about her little daughter.

With the frequent postings that were a feature of Elizabeth's early life, they were not to enjoy Avor for very long. In May of the following year they moved to Auxonne, and Mme. Catez began to discover that her lively and beautiful daughter was fast developing a ferocious temper and a strength of will that would tax hers to the limit.

When Elizabeth was nineteen months old, Mme. Rolland fell seriously ill, and Mme. Catez had to hurry south to be with her mother. The Rollands had returned to the Aude region on Commandant

Rolland's retirement from the army and settled in Saint-Hilaire, where the commandant was now tax inspector for the region. Mme. Catez took Elizabeth with her, and while they were staying there, a mission was held. It ended with a special service of blessing for the children. One of the sisters organizing it came to ask if she could use Elizabeth's favorite doll, Jeanette, as the little baby Jesus in the crib. It was hoped that she wouldn't recognize her doll if it was dressed in a robe covered with gold stars.

This was to underestimate Elizabeth's intelligence. At first she was distracted by all the people arriving for the service, but then, as the priest announced the blessing from the pulpit, she glanced at the crib, recognized Jeanette and, her eyes blazing with rage, demanded loudly, "Jeanette! Give me back my Jeanette!" The congregation collapsed into laughter as her embarrassed nurse hurried her out of the church (RB 1:2–3; LLL 27).

The photographs taken at this time show her precious doll clasped firmly in her arms, and they also show those flashing dark eyes that could so easily blaze with temper. But she was also revealing another side of herself, her love for God. On their return to Auxonne, Mme. Catez kept her mother up to date with news of Elizabeth in a series of letters that reveal these various facets of her character. "She went up at the Offertory and kissed the Crucifix," Mme. Catez wrote, and "she was throwing kisses to it before she got there. 'She not only prays' for her sick grandmother 'but she is teaching her doll how to pray; she has just very devoutly made her kneel'" (Works, v. 1, p. 8). But "she is a real devil," Mme. Catez commented in another letter. "She is crawling and needs a fresh pair of pants every day.... [Her] fine prattling will amuse you very much; she is a big chatterbox" (RB 1:2–3; LLL 26).

Mme. Catez wrote to her parents at the end of April 1882 and guided Elizabeth's hand to add a few words of her own:

> Dear Mama Line and Papa Mond,
> Thank you for the oranges. I pray to the good Jesus for
> Line who has bobo [her word for Mme. Roland's illness].
> I kiss you. (L 1)

Barely a week after receiving these letters, Mme. Rolland died, and the commandant came to live with them. Then in November, Captain Catez received a new posting, and the whole family moved to Dijon, where they settled in the Rue Lamartine. It must have been a very stressful time for Mme. Catez, because she was also six months pregnant. On February 20 her second daughter was born, whom they named Marguerite. Fortunately for their mother, Sabeth and Guite, as they were nicknamed, were totally opposite in character. Guite was as quiet and gentle as Sabeth was quick-tempered and lively, and Elizabeth's temper was getting worse. Guite remembered that she was quite terrible when she went into one of her rages; "she was a real little devil" (LLL 33). On one occasion she shut herself into a room and stamped and raged, kicking at the door until her temper subsided. Another time her mother packed a small bag for Elizabeth and threatened to send her off to the Good Shepherd nuns, who ran a house of correction nearby.

Mme. Catez had other worries to contend with as well; Captain Catez was beginning to suffer from heart trouble, and when he was away she worried about his health. "Do not forget my advice; take care of yourself; do not drink too much beer or smoke too many cigars; take care of your health and think of us," she wrote to him on April 28, 1885 (Works, v. 1, p. 9). Five commands in a few lines: this was undoubtedly where Elizabeth inherited her imperiousness; she inherited her love of life and her friendliness from her father.

While he was away, Mme. Catez kept her husband up to date with news of the children: "The little ones are more or less well behaved, Elizabeth often thinks and speaks of you; she is counting the days," she continued in the same letter. By this time Elizabeth was old enough to write a short letter of her own to go with her mother's, and Jeanette was obviously still her favorite toy:

> My little Papa, it is very kind of you to think of my dolls.
> A little crocheted bonnet for my doll would please me a
> lot. I am finding the time very long without you, and I
> send a kiss to you and my cousins. (L 2)

Elizabeth did not have long to wait to see him, though, for his health was continuing to deteriorate, and in June of that year he retired from the army.

The family had two happy years together; they were a very happy and united family. Commandant Rolland proved to be an excellent grandfather and an accomplished storyteller. The two girls would climb up on his knee, and he could keep them amused for hours. There was a very strong bond between the two of them despite their very disparate characters, and Elizabeth was just as passionate in expressing her love as she was in showing her temper.

As they had settled down in Dijon, they were able to make an established circle of friends in the town, mostly among other army families. Their neighbors, the Gumards, were already friends; there was the Chervau family who lived in the Rue de Mirande whose daughter Alice, nearly two years older than Elizabeth, was one of her best friends. Above all, there was the Hallo family with whom they were in almost daily contact. Commandant and Mme. Hallo had two children: Marie-Louise, who was just a month older than Elizabeth; and Charles, who was two years younger. Elizabeth called Mme. Hallo her "second mother," and Marie-Louise was Elizabeth's best friend. The two families always kept very close ties with each other.

The children were very fortunate in having a large park nearby to play in and the lovely countryside to explore, and Elizabeth was always the leader in thinking up new things to do. Every year, too, there were trips to visit the friends they had made in their various postings as well as visits to their widely scattered relatives.

This period of happiness was to be shattered, though, when Commandant Rolland died on January 24, 1887. Then Captain Catez, who had already suffered several heart attacks, died suddenly on Sunday, October 2. He was fifty-four.

Elizabeth was with him when he died, and ten years later she commemorated his death in a poem.

> It was in my weak child's arms
> Those arms that hugged you so

That your brief agony lasted,
Your life's last fight.
I tried to hold on to
That last, long sigh. (P 37)

Captain Catez had been highly respected by all who knew him, and the funeral orations and newspaper obituaries paid tribute to his integrity, his nobility of character, and the affection in which he had been held by all. He had been awarded the Military Medal and had been made a Chevalier of the Legion of Honor on January 18, 1881. Captain Chézelle, who gave the main funeral oration, summed it up with the greatest simplicity and truth when he called him this "excellent Christian" (Works, v.1, p. 10).

His death meant great changes for Mme. Catez and the two children—the "trio" as they called themselves now. Mme. Catez had to live on a much reduced pension, although they were still comfortably off. But they no longer needed the large house in the Rue Lamartine and very soon moved into a smaller house in the Rue Prieur de la Côte d'Or.

There was also Elizabeth's education to think of. She was now seven years old, and as soon as they had settled into their new home, Mme. Catez arranged for her to have French lessons at home with Mlle. Grémaux. She also began to have instructions in preparation for her first confession.

Elizabeth called her first confession her "conversion"; the experience gave her a jolt that awakened her to the divine. So, too, the deaths of two people so dear to her and the upheaval of moving house must have made her realize that her temper tantrums were making her mother's grief and burdens even more difficult for her to cope with. Elizabeth resolved to try and take herself in hand and, with her strong will, the results were soon evident, although she had a long battle ahead.

Once they had settled into their new house, Mme. Catez took the girls on holiday for a few weeks. They stayed at the army camp at Châlons, enjoying the military maneuvers and reviews, and went to the Rollands' hometown of Saint-Hilaire to spend some time with an old family friend of theirs, Canon Angles, who was the parish priest there.

One evening the two girls were playing; at one point Elizabeth left their games and climbed up on Canon Angles's knee. Very solemnly she bent his head toward her and whispered her big secret into his ear. "Canon, I'm going to be a nun, I want to be a nun!" She didn't whisper softly enough, though, because her mother overheard her. "What's the silly little thing saying?" she asked sharply. She was sufficiently worried to seek Canon Angles out the following day in the cloister of the Benedictine abbey nearby. She asked him if he believed Elizabeth's vocation was genuine. Canon Angles had known Elizabeth since she was a baby. He had the discernment to see beneath the temper tantrums to the deep integrity of her character. Her parish priest was to remark that "Elizabeth, with her temperament, will be either an angel or a devil." Canon Angles was already aware of the presence of God within her and was able to say to Mme. Catez with utter conviction, "Yes, I do!" (Souv. 14–15).

It was the last thing Mme. Catez wanted to hear. She herself, after her fiancé's death in the War of 1870, had toyed with the idea of a religious vocation. She loved the writings of St. Teresa of Avila but couldn't bear the thought of Elizabeth entering religious life.

Still, Elizabeth was only seven years old. At that time many children of her age dreamt of becoming nuns, but few actually did so. She could only hope Elizabeth would forget about it in the days ahead. In the meantime, there was plenty to occupy her mind on their return to Dijon. There were, for example, a series of concerts being organized for young children, and Mme. Catez entered Elizabeth to play the piano. She performed Steibelt's *L'Orage* with a brilliant and expressive style that drew the judges' attention to her. People came up to Elizabeth afterward to congratulate her, but she turned to her mother, "How did I play my piece?"

Mme. Catez hesitated, worried that all the praise would go to her head. "It was all right," she said.

"I'll try harder next time," replied Elizabeth. Her mother's opinion meant more to her than praise from others (Souv. 8).

Elizabeth's obvious musical gifts encouraged Mme. Catez to enroll her in the Conservatory of Dijon that October to study the piano, probably to prepare her for a career as a piano teacher. Her days would now be filled with music lessons and long hours of piano practice. There were the usual lessons at the Conservatory, of course, and private lessons at home, but other subjects invariably received less attention. Her general education, therefore, was somewhat sketchy, and her grammar and spelling would always follow rules of their own.

For Elizabeth herself, though, the most important thing ahead was her First Communion, some eighteen months away; she was already preparing herself for that great day. Her closest friends would notice that, without dampening her sense of fun and high spirits, she would press her lips together to hold back an angry reply when told off; or if they were planning things to do, Elizabeth would hold back on her own ideas to give others a chance. Above all, they noticed her love of prayer. However boisterous she was normally, when she was in church, she would immediately quiet down and remain motionless in prayer.

She wrote a letter to her mother for the New Year 1889, which shows her clear-sighted realism and the sense of humor she brought to her program of reformation; she firmly hedged her bets on how successful she would be:

> Darling little Mother,
> I want to wish you a good New Year and promise you I will be very good, very obedient, and I won't make you angry again, I won't cry anymore, and I'll be a little model to please you, but you may not believe me. I'll do my best to keep my promises so I won't have told a lie in my letter as I sometimes have. I had a long, long letter in my head, but I can't remember anymore! You'll see, though, that I will be very good. (L 4)

She seemed to have had some success during the year, though, for her letter for the next year showed her making the same resolutions, but not hedging her bets so much:

I'm so pleased to see the New Year and to renew my promises for a good year. I wish you all you can desire, and now that I am more grown up, I'm going to be a very gentle little girl, patient, obedient, conscientious, and not falling into tempers. And since I'm the elder I must set my sister a good example; I won't quarrel with her anymore, but I'll be such a little model that you'll be able to say you are the happiest of mothers, and since I hope to have the happiness of making my First Communion soon, I will be even more well-behaved, and I'll pray to God to make me even better. (L 5)

During this time Marguerite, showing a similar musical talent, joined Elizabeth at the Conservatory, and the family continued to enjoy their long summer holidays with their friends and relatives. Canon Angles remembered Sabeth and Guite with their band of friends going on energetic hikes in the lovely countryside. "I can see her now," he recalled, "on our walks among the mountains, woods, and fields, crossing the rivers, always at the head of the group. Only her mother, with a look or a word, could calm her exuberance." Guite, on the other hand, was shy, retiring, and so serious that he nicknamed her "Justice."

One worrisome incident that happened at this time, perhaps on their holidays, was that Mme. Catez became seriously ill from a snakebite. It affected her so much that it changed her complexion and her features; it permanently affected her health. A photograph taken when she was forty-four shows her looking much older.

At home in Dijon Elizabeth's thoughts were more and more occupied by the prospect of her First Communion and the growing call of God within her. She loved organizing her friends to play nuns with her, something that alarmed her mother. At last the time came for her to join the catechism class in preparation for her First Communion. But her efforts to prepare for Jesus' coming to her did not quell her high spirits during the classes. One day during a walk, her exasperated parish priest was driven to making her and her friend kneel down on the pavement until they behaved themselves.

2

JESUS HAS FED ME
First Communion

The day of Elizabeth's First Communion, April 19, 1891, arrived at last. Captain Chaboisseau, the chaplain at Avor who had baptized Elizabeth, came to concelebrate the Mass with the parish priest, Abbé Sauvageot. He had a long talk with Elizabeth the evening before. He was deeply impressed with the depth of her love for God, realizing that it was much more than simple childhood fervor.

Elizabeth herself testified that even before making her First Communion, she had such a love of God and of prayer that it was inconceivable to her that she could give her heart fully to anyone but God.

She made her First Communion in the imposing parish church of St. Michael. She was dressed in a long white dress and veil, stud earrings, a mother of pearl cross, and a gold medal of Our Lady. In her white-gloved hands she held a beautiful, gilt-edged hand missal and a blue rosary with a silver cross, all gifts from her family and friends.

Tears of joy streamed down her face as she received the Lord's body for the first time. Seven years later she commemorated the day in a poem that gives a small glimpse of what it meant to her:

> On that day
> When Jesus made his home in me,
> When God took possession of my heart,
> So completely, so well, that since that hour,
> Since that secret interchange,
> That divine, delightful intercourse,
> my one desire has been to give my life,
> To repay some little way his mighty love,
> To the Beloved of the Eucharist
> Who lives within my feeble heart,
> Flooding it with his favors....
> The most beautiful day of my life. (P 47)

13

She recognized the debt she owed to her mother, too, for preparing her and wrote later: "If I love Him a little, it is you who directed the heart of your little one toward Him. You prepared me so well for that first encounter, that great day when we gave ourselves totally to one another..." (L 178).

"I will never forget the emotions of that day," Mme. Catez recalled in her turn. "I saw my child so absorbed, so overwhelmed, tears never stopped falling, that I understood that God had taken possession of a heart that was so pure and loving."

Marie-Louise Hallo made her First Communion with her, and as they walked down the steps together afterward, Elizabeth whispered to her, "I'm not hungry, Jesus has fed me..." (Souv. 9).

Later that day Elizabeth, still in her white dress, went to the Discalced Carmelite monastery just around the corner. In the austere parlor with its forbidding grilles, she was introduced to the prioress, Mother Marie of Jesus, by Mme. de Vathaire, a mutual friend of both the Catez family and the community.

Marie of Jesus was at this time thirty-eight years old and had been elected prioress for the first time about eighteen months previously. She had been in Carmel for nineteen years, a woman of great intelligence, charm, and depth of spirituality. She was large-hearted with a joyful spirit that drew others to the Lord she loved, a Carmelite after Teresa of Avila's own heart.

She testified later that her first meeting with Elizabeth made a lasting impression on her. As a souvenir of Elizabeth's First Communion, Marie of Jesus gave her a prayer card of sayings of St. Teresa of Avila. Around the edge she wrote a short poem of her own, explaining the meaning of Elizabeth's name—House of God.

> Your blessed name holds a mystery
> Fulfilled this great day.
> Child, your heart, here on earth,
> Is the House of the God of Love. (Souv. 9)

Elizabeth kept it carefully in her prayer book for the rest of her life. Marie of Jesus said she had no idea then how important that doctrine of the indwelling of God was to be for Elizabeth. It was a mystery that Elizabeth had already experienced earlier that day. She had no words as yet to explain it, but the profound change in her from that day on expressed it far more clearly than any words.

Two months later she put on her white dress once more for her Confirmation, which took place on June 8 in the church of Notre Dame in Dijon, and then the family was off once more for their long summer holidays.

A photograph taken not long afterward, in which she is wearing the earrings and a chaplet given her for her First Communion, shows the change already taking place in her. Beneath the straight eyebrows, her dark eyes no longer have the angry expression they once did. They are round and clear with a sweetness and directness of expression about her that is a lovely witness to the Spirit at work in her.

Canon Angles was impressed by the change and admired the energy she showed in keeping a balance between the two poles of passion and tenderness that characterized her. Nobody realized how hard the struggle often was, and the only sign that sometimes betrayed her would be the glint of tears beneath her eyelashes.

She spoke rarely of her inner life, even to those closest to her. Her friends knew her more for her high-spirited gaiety, which was increasingly tempered by a tranquil self-control that made her more sensitive to the needs of others. She loved going to parties, as her parish priest noticed, but a friend later remembered how her love for God affected her concern for others.

> We first met at a children's party; I was only ten years old and felt very intimidated when I heard all the noise of the other children behind the door when it was opened to us. Going in I was immediately struck by Elizabeth, who I soon realized was the heart and soul of the party. It didn't take long for me to get to know and appreciate her. I was very lively and hotheaded, and I was amazed at how even-tempered and gentle she was. I envied the way she was so calm and in control of herself, always ready to put herself in the background and to give way to others. When I realized that such self-possession wasn't her natural character but the result of grace, my envy changed to profound

admiration, and I realized I would have to follow her example. (Souv. 22)

As her friend realized, it was the result of grace, not nature. As much as she enjoyed parties, Elizabeth would spend some time in prayer in her room beforehand, asking God to watch over her and keep her inwardly united with him. This was the keynote of her inner life at this time, that she wanted, in the words of St. Catherine of Siena, to make an inner cell within herself where she could keep her Lord company and, even in the midst of her daily life, keep her heart and her thoughts fixed on him.

A simple logic flowing from this made itself apparent in many small ways. One day she was going past a theater, for example, and exclaimed, "Oh, I'd love to be an actress!"

Guite remembered that they looked at her in astonishment. "You, an actress?"

"Yes," she replied, "because then there would be at least one person there who loved God" (Souv. 19). If God was with her and in her, then wherever she was, God was too.

God was in her music as well. On her thirteenth birthday she won the First Prize for Excellence at the Conservatory, and a week later on the July 25, won First Prize at the piano. The local newspaper, *Le Progrès de la Côte d'Or*, reported it in glowing terms on August 8, 1893:

> Mlle. Catez, first prize at the piano, of M. Diétrich's class, received unanimous applause after the *Capriccio Brillant* of Mendelssohn. It was a pleasure to see this young child of scarcely thirteen years old come to the piano; she is already a distinguished pianist with an excellent touch, a beautiful tone, and a real musical feeling. A debut like this permits us to base great hopes on this child. (Works, v. 1, p. 13)

Much later she revealed the secret of her self-possession and musical sensitivity in a letter to Madeleine, a young friend of hers who was nervous at the thought of playing in public:

I shall pray for Madeleine that God may be even in her
little fingertips; then I shall defy anyone to rival her. She
shouldn't be nervous; I'm going to tell her my secret: to
forget her audience and imagine she is alone with the divine Master; then she will play for him with all her heart
and bring out of her instrument full, yet strong and sweet,
sound. How I used to love doing this! (Souv. 24)

She felt an increasing hunger for prayer, and if it was left to her,
would have spent hours before the Blessed Sacrament. The Eucharist
was at the center of her life, and the tears would often stream down
her face as she received Communion. All this was the work of grace
but also of her strong will and determination, and when she was about
thirteen, her continual efforts to make herself pleasing to God resulted
in a period of scruples. She was not helped by the Jansenistic tenden-
cies of the time that her mother shared to some extent, which emphasized God as a stern judge who demanded perfection from his
followers. There was also a sometimes morbid obsession with suffering, mortification, and death in the spirituality of the time that also
influenced her and could easily have contributed to her inner darkness at this time.

Fortunately, though, she had a very positive spirit and common
sense that brought her through this difficult period; she was helped,
too, by her parish priest, Abbé Sauvageot. He brought her gently back
to the awareness—far more instinctive to her—of a God of infinite
and tender love who only wanted her total love in return.

A love of suffering and an intense desire to die young remained
with her, though; she longed to die but was afraid of the judgment, a
prospect that often kept her awake and fearful at night. When she
recovered her awareness of God's love again, however, it drove out
this fear, leaving her with a luminous longing for heaven. So much
did she desire heaven that when she was fourteen, she persuaded a
friend of hers, Louise Recoing, to go with her at Easter time to the
shrine of Notre Dame d'Etang in Burgundy, where she prayed for the
grace to die young. Often the Lord inspires us to pray for that which
he wills to give us, and early on he was preparing Elizabeth for what
was to come.

Her love of suffering, too, was purged of any morbidity. She desired it not for itself, but because her Master had suffered and died for her, and it was one way of repaying his love; it was also a way of winning souls, of drawing others to love him too. So Elizabeth's natural enjoyment of life had returned by the time the family set off for their holidays in the summer of 1893 after her triumphs at the Conservatory.

They stayed a fortnight at Gemeaux with the Comtesse de Sourdon, a close friend of Mme. Catez whom Elizabeth called her second mother—she seemed to have quite a few of them. Sabeth and Guite became very close friends with the Sourdon girls, Marie-Louise and Françoise. Françoise, whom Elizabeth nicknamed "Framboise" (Raspberry) was some eight years younger than herself. They were also friendly with the Gemeaux family, who lived in a chateau a short distance from the Sourdons, with two girls, Germaine and Yvonne, and a son Albert.

Together they played endless games of croquet and had energetic walks in the lovely countryside. They also went to the Gemeaux chateau often, where Elizabeth would play the piano. Monsieur de Gemeaux was very fond of music and had a beautiful deep voice; Elizabeth had enduring memories of many hours accompanying him on the piano. Her playing moved him so deeply that he sometimes had tears in his eyes.

They spent two weeks at Gemeaux with Mme. de Sourdon, who didn't want them to leave, and then went on to see friends in Mirecourt. There they were feted with enormous meals in their honor that left them groaning.

From there they traveled to the Jura, where they went on long excursions into the surrounding countryside that Elizabeth loved. "I love the beautiful pine forests so much," she wrote to her friend, Alice Chervau. "We went to the source of the Ain, to the Mailly waterfall, to Noseroy, to pick raspberries in the woods. We spend our days exploring the countryside and the good country air is doing us good" (L 6).

The holidays came to an end, though, and in October the two girls went back to the Conservatory. Inwardly Elizabeth was more and more preoccupied with her call to the religious life. Just before her four-teenth birthday, she was making her thanksgiving after Mass when she felt irresistibly drawn to choose Jesus as her only spouse, and she immediately bound herself to him by a vow of virginity.

"We didn't say anything to each other," she wrote afterward, "but we gave ourselves to each other with such intense love that my determination to be wholly his became even stronger" (Souv. 18–19).

At this point she was drawn to the Trappistine order with its emphasis on silence, which she felt was stricter than the Carmelites. But a short while after she made her vow of virginity, again during her thanksgiving after Mass, she heard the word "Carmel" uttered deep within her. From this point on, she said that her one ambition was to be behind Carmel's grilles. Later that day, during a quiet break in a lively game of croquet, she confided what had happened to one of her friends.

So intense was her longing that the waiting was hard for her. A family friend, seeing her look pensive and somewhat sad one day, went up to her and asked her why she was looking so dismal when there was so much in her life to make her happy. "I'm thinking how happy I'll be when Carmel opens its doors to me," she replied. "The time seems to pass so slowly, and I want to be in God's service straight away."

"I laughed at this premature decision," added the friend, pointing out that she could love and serve God in the world and look after her devoted mother. "She let me finish, then replied that 'God wants me for himself. My darling mother will understand my desire, and she'll be glad when I leave her, knowing my happiness. And I'll love her just as much.'"

With Carmel taking up so much of her thoughts, she wasn't affected quite as much as she could have been by the sour note on which the year at the Conservatory ended. Elizabeth was once again awarded the Prize for Excellence, but this time it was taken away from her in circumstances she described to her friend Alice Chervau.

"There has been a great deal of excitement at the Conservatory on my account," she wrote once when the family had set off on their holidays.

> The board unanimously awarded me a prize, but M. Fritsch, whose pupil had already won one, felt I would tarnish his pupil's glory; he ran to the prefecture, as did Mme. Vendeur. They did so well that the Prefecture agreed with them and said the Board didn't have the right to award the prize to me. Then the Board members, very upset, wanted to resign, and if M. Deroye, the president of the board, had been notified, things wouldn't have turned out as they did, for he would have gone to the prefect, so he told M. Lévêque.... So you've no idea of the fuss, and M. Fritsch was the cause of it all; such a silly way to go about it; he is annoyed with M. Diétrich. (L 7)

There was one bright note about it all: Guite won second prize at the piano. But the family was glad to leave the unpleasantness of the affair behind and revel in the peace of the Midi and Carlipa. They always spent alternate years in the Midi, staying with Mme. Catez's aunt, Catherine Rolland, and her uncle, François, who was to die later that year on October 2. They had two unmarried daughters, Mathilde, who was hard of hearing, and Francine, who had bad eyesight. Elizabeth always referred to them as her aunts as they were so much older than she, although they were in fact her cousins.

She was very fond of her "Rolland aunts" and loved the peace of Carlipa. It is a small village nestling on the south side of the Serre, a hill with a wide-plateaued top and the backdrop of the Pyrenees in the far distance. Years later in Carmel, she would recall fondly the walks they took on the Serre on moonlit evenings, the bells from the small village church ringing a carillon into the starlit sky. During the day the family would go down to spend time by the sea nearby, walk in the thickly wooded countryside, or follow the river Lampy through its lovely valley, and return to be coddled by their cousins, doing honor to their excellent southern cooking.

Morning and evening she would go with her aunts to the little church to pray; the side chapel had a marble altar and a statue of Our Lady, both donated by the family. Elizabeth also loved to play the harmonium there. An important date this year was August 11, when she first started writing her verse. So far all that remains from this period, apart from her verse, is a prayer she wrote on April 22, 1894, to her patron Saint Elizabeth of Hungary:

> Remember, Saint Elizabeth, my patron and my protectress, that I am your little charge. Come to help me here on this barren earth and help me in my weakness. Give me your lovely virtues, your gentle humility, and your high charity. Grant for me that God will change my faults to virtues as he changed the bread you carried to roses. May I fly to heaven on the wings of hope; then, when God calls me to himself, do you yourself receive me at the gate of heaven. (Souv. 10)

About the same time she wrote a short poem to Our Lady on the back cover of one of her music notebooks:

> Mary, tender Mother,
> I put myself in your care.
> Hear my prayer,
> And bless my resolutions. (P 1)

She may have started writing her diaries about this period, but just before entering Carmel she burned all of them but one, so the verses she started writing while at Carlipa are the only record of her inner life at this period. They have almost no literary value, but they form a precious record of her spiritual preoccupations. There are verses to her mother, to Guite, to friends, and relatives. She wrote verses about the various places they visited, such as, Saint-Martin:

> Near to an eternal rock,
> Lifting my heart to heaven,
> There by the river bank
> I love to pray. (P 5)

There are verses to the Bassin de Lampy, to the sea. The beauties around her always reminded her heart of heaven. But there is also a poem to Jesus that sets out her spiritual concern very concisely:

Jesus, for you my soul is jealous,
I want soon to be your spouse.
With you I want to suffer,
And, to find you, die. (P 4)

Here is her yearning to suffer with Jesus, her longing for death (using
Saint Teresa's saying "to suffer or to die," which Elizabeth made thor-
oughly her own at this period), and her consciousness of her call to
the religious life, themes that she returned to in other poems too. In
her verses she speaks in the accepted language of the period about the
miseries of life, but her far more natural inclination comes out in those
verses that express her appreciation of the beauty around her, the lovely
scenery that lifted her heart to the God who created it, verses that
speak of love, given and received, for her family and friends. It was
only in that awareness of heaven that so engaged her heart that lesser
things shone more dimly.

At last it was time to leave Carlipa, "that little corner of heaven /
Where I first made my verse" (P 8), as Elizabeth recorded, to return to
Dijon and further studies at the Conservatory.

Elizabeth, almost 11, in her First Communion dress holding her missal. The photograph was not taken on the day of her First Communion, April 19, 1891, since the roses in the background would not yet be in bloom. Most likely it was taken on her Confirmation day, June 8, since the children wore their First Communion clothes for Confirmation also.

Elizabeth at the piano in August 1893. In July she had been awarded first prize for piano at the Conservatory of Dijon.

3

ELIZABETH OF THE BIG FEET
Teenage Years

Elizabeth had gone as far as she could with her piano studies at the Dijon Conservatory; if she wanted to continue, she would need to go to the Paris Conservatory. It was decided that she would stay in Dijon and take a further two years of harmony instead. In addition, perhaps concerned that their general education was not keeping up with their music studies, Mme. Catez engaged a new teacher for the two girls, Mlle. Irma Forey. She was too easygoing, though, and their studies had been too neglected for them to improve.

In an attempt to get to know her new pupils better, toward the end of November Mlle. Forey gave them an essay to write—to describe their physical and moral portrait. Elizabeth tackled the assignment with a light touch that revealed almost nothing of her inner life:

> To draw one's physical and moral portrait is a delicate subject to deal with, but taking my courage in both hands I set to work and begin!
> Without pride I think that I can say that my overall appearance is not displeasing. I am a brunette and, they say, rather tall for my age. I have sparkling black eyes and my thick eyebrows give me a severe look. The rest of my person is insignificant. My "dainty" feet could win for me the nickname of Elizabeth of the Big Feet, like Queen Bertha! And there you have my physical portrait!
> As for my moral portrait, I would say that I have a rather good character. I am cheerful and, I must confess, somewhat scatterbrained. I have a good heart. I am by nature a coquette. "One should be a little!" they say. I am not lazy: I know "work makes us happy." Without being a model of patience, I usually know how to control myself. I do not hold grudges. So much for my moral portrait. I have my defects and, alas, few good qualities! I hope to acquire them!

Well, at last this tedious task is finished and am I glad.
(Works, v. 1, p. 13)

Her friends agreed that she wasn't pretty in the accepted sense.
She normally wore her thick, dark brown, waist-length hair caught
back to hang loose or in a long plait. According to Françoise de
Sourdon, her mouth was too large and her nose turned up a bit
too much. However everyone agreed that there was a luminosity about
her that made her special. Above all, it was her incomparable
dark eyes. "She had a look about her," said Antoinette de Bobet, "her
smile! What I still see is that radiance, that look. I felt as if she could
see right through me" (LLL 9). It was above all when she was
in prayer, or returning from Holy Communion, that her expression
was unforgettable.

Already, by the age of fourteen, she could in all honesty say that
self-control, rather than lack of patience, was characteristic of her.
Her temper tantrums were long a thing of the past, although perhaps
only she knew how her blood could boil at an occasional slight or
injustice, and that she would need all her self-control to bite back an
impatient or angry word. Only the most observant of her friends noticed her self-denial, so graciously and unobtrusively did she practice
it, eating whatever was given to her, giving way to the wishes of others. One of her friends testified that no one ever remembered her saying anything bad about anyone, or anything good that wasn't true
(Souv. 24–25; LLL 51).

She was most appreciated not only for her kindness and thoughtfulness toward others but also for her tremendous drive, her sense of
fun. "She did not love the world but she was in it and seemed to enjoy
herself" (EP 4:2–9; LLL 9), summed up Françoise.

The year at the Conservatory ended with Guite taking First Prize
for the piano, and Elizabeth winning a prize for harmony. It was an
exceptionally hot and humid summer, and they were glad to get away
from Dijon to the Midi where, in the refreshing air of the pine woods
of Mirecourt, they had some respite from the heat.

They spent a longer period at Champagnole with their old friends
the Hallos. "Every day we set out as tourists," Elizabeth recorded in

the diary she kept of the holidays, "either by carriage or on foot, for we have excellent legs and are not frightened by 20 kilometers" (CE 30; LLL 42). Charles, a year and a half younger than the two eldest girls, Marie-Louise and Elizabeth, must have felt somewhat overwhelmed by the female company and ended up arguing with Elizabeth on one of their trips. She was very fond of him, though, the "little brother" she and Guite didn't have themselves.

The next year was Elizabeth's last at the Conservatory. Guite won First Prize for Excellence with reviews in the local paper calling her a little prodigy. Then they were off once more on their holidays with a packed itinerary that she described in a letter to Alice Chervau:

> We have arrived safely in Carlipa, less tired than mother feared. We stopped for four hours in Lyon, time to make a pilgrimage to Fourvières, which was crowded. The basilica is splendid; Lyon has lavished all her wealth on it. Leaving Fourvières we dined at a restaurant in the open air, then at 8 o'clock we left for Cette, where we arrived at five o'clock in the morning. We spent our morning on the beach admiring the sea that I love so much and watching the bathers. By four o'clock we were in Carlipa, where my cousins pampered and fussed over us, and we did honor to the excellent Midi cuisine. We are having some marvelous walks; only after a storm the temperature is so fresh that it is almost cold. (L 9)

"I have put my hair up," she added in a postscript, "and it has made me look very grown-up." Suddenly, she was a young woman.

From Carlipa they went to Saint-Hilaire to see Canon Angles and were given such enormous meals that their stomachs begged for mercy, then to Limoux, where she met another of her friends, Gabrielle Montpellier. "She is twenty years old and charming," wrote Elizabeth to Alice.

> We are having some wonderful trips into the country. Tomorrow we are going to spend the day at Ginoles-les-Bains, and we are looking forward to it immensely.... I am making lots of music here; my friend has an excellent baby grand that is my delight; it has a superb tone, and I

could spend hours at it. I accompany Gabrielle's cousin
who plays the violin very well; her husbandis an excellent pianist and we sight read for four hands. (L 11)

There was also a visit to Lourdes, probably the second time she had
been there, and they returned to Dijon at the end of October.
What she didn't mention in her letters was her increasing homesickness for Carmel. It was only in her poems, which she called "the
echo of my heart," that she was able to express her longings for the
solitude of Carmel, for a cloister hard and austere (P 29). The Dijon
Carmel was just around the corner from their house, and from her
bedroom window Elizabeth was able to see part of the garden, a stately
avenue of trees with glimpses of sisters working or praying in the
garden, and drink in every detail of their monastic dress. In the quiet
of the evening as the Angelus rang, she would step out onto her bal-
cony to join in their prayer, and she could see the long rows of small
windows that were the sisters' cells. She loved all this, but at the same
time it was tantalizing to have Carmel so near, and yet so far.

On three days of February 1897, three clothings took place, which
Elizabeth attended and described in a poem, noting every detail:

> The gentle chimes of Carmel
> Mount slowly to heaven.
> The altar is adorned with flowers
> Releasing their sweet fragrance.
> The candles shine everywhere,
> Making it a corner of heaven.
> All at once, in her bridal robe,
> The gentle bride appears.
> Her face is pure and radiant,
> Her joy is painted in her eyes.
> She is perhaps happy and proud,
> For the moment now is come
> When she gives herself completely
> To her beloved Jesus,
> Her heavenly spouse,
> The gentle judge.
> Soon at the monastery door
> She goes and gently knocks
> And veiled figures with an austere air

Come and open to her, singing.
At the foot of a great crucifix,
This confidant, this heavenly friend,
His bride kneels,
And gives her heart to her divine Spouse.
Then, saying farewell to those she loves on earth,
She disappears to live alone
With these elite souls,
A pure and humble Carmelite. (P 31)

Elizabeth would often slip into the chapel at Carmel to pray or to go to Mass; she could talk sometimes to the extern sisters with perhaps an occasional visit to the parlor. Seeing the sisters at close quarters, she could take in every detail of the coarse brown habit, the big wooden rosary with its simple crucifix, the white mantle, the leather belt, and she longed for the time when she would be clothed in them all, when she would have a bare cell with its bed of boards herself.

Her confessor, Abbé Sellenet, left Dijon around this time to take up another post; he had long been convinced that Elizabeth's vocation was genuine, and before he left, he spoke with her mother, urging her not to oppose Elizabeth's call to the cloister. Unfortunately, his intervention had the opposite effect and, alarmed by the thought that she really could lose Elizabeth, Mme. Catez forbade her to make any more visits to Carmel. This was an enormous blow to Elizabeth, but one she obeyed without question. In her poems she expressed her longing to suffer with and for her Master, and there could be no greater sacrifice for her than this.

What she could do, though, was to steep herself in the writings of Saint Teresa of Avila and absorb the Carmelite spirit. Her poems of this period drew their inspiration quite heavily from St. Teresa's writings; ironically, she used her mother's own treasured copies of St. Teresa's works. Prayer was becoming habitual to her, as natural and necessary as breathing:

My heart is always with him,
And night and day it thinks
Of that divine and heavenly Friend
To whom it wants to prove its tenderness. (P 43)

She wanted to keep herself pure for him, to do what pleased him, and to suffer long for him on behalf of others. This bare recitation sums up the basis of her spiritual life, and from it springs the richness of her mystical life.

The asceticism implied in this poem was lived out unobtrusively in the social round and the enjoyment of their extended holidays. In 1898 they stayed at Tarbes, which, as Elizabeth wrote, was one long round of pleasures: with a wide circle of friends she attended dances, played and listened to music, and went on trips to the countryside. It was only in an unguarded moment during a party while she was dancing and having a good time that Mme. d'Avout caught a faraway look in her eyes and whispered to her, "Elizabeth, you are not here, you see God." Elizabeth smiled at her without speaking (AP 648; LLL 9).

From Tarbes they went on to Lourdes, that corner of heaven where Elizabeth was able to pray and receive Communion at the Grotto for three days. From her description it was far different from today. "They don't have big pilgrimages," she wrote to Valentine Defougues, "I love the calm of Lourdes" (L 15).

They then went on to Pau to visit Henri IV's chateau with its superb tapestries and then took the glorious scenic route via Cauterets and Pierrefit to Luchon. All of them were overwhelmed by the splendor of the mountain scenery, which Elizabeth said she was crazy about and that she never wanted to leave. But Luchon, "Queen of the Pyrenees," was even more breathtaking. They spent two days there, which enabled them to meet up with some Rostang cousins and, with Canon Angles, take a landau drawn by four horses to the "Gulf of Hell," some 1,800 meters up the mountain. To the terror of the rest of the party, Elizabeth and a young friend, Madeleine Guémard, pranced around the edge of the awesome ravine, completely unaffected by the enormous drop plunging to the waters below (L 15).

After Luchon, though, it was on to dear Carlipa, which Elizabeth loved so much, and before whose peaceful serenity even the splendors of the Pyrenees faded. Her contemplative spirit was deeply at home in the quiet tranquillity of the country life she loved. They returned to Dijon via Marseille, the Grand Chartreuse, Annecy, Grenoble, and Geneva. At Marseille they went on board a transatlantic liner, when once again she gave evidence of her strong stomach and nerves; she was not affected by an extremely rough crossing in the small boat that took them out to the ship. At the Grande Chartreuse she was able to appreciate the depth of the silence that enveloped the famous abbey, deep in its magnificent countryside of richly wooded mountains. They stayed in a small convent close by the abbey, each having a cell to sleep in, with atrociously hard beds. At Annecy they stayed with a friend of Mme. Catez and were able to tour the picturesque lake (L 18).

Mme. Catez hoped that she might persuade Elizabeth to change her mind by having her experience some of the beauty of the world that she was so intent on leaving. In this she failed. Elizabeth, in the words of Scripture, was charmed by their beauty but knew how much the Lord of these excelled them, since the very Author of beauty has created them (Wisdom 13:3). All that she saw simply raised her mind and heart to their Creator and made her long for the sight of the One whose beauty was far beyond what she saw. But it did provide her with a rich store of memories and experiences when she was within the cloister that she loved far more than the world.

4

A BIT OF A COQUETTE
Life in the World

On their return to Dijon there was a whole round of reunions and parties for the two girls to attend. Guite had finished her studies at the Conservatory that year, and their lessons with Mlle. Forey also ended. However, Mme. Catez thought it would be a good idea for them to learn English and engaged a young English woman, Alice Skelton, to give them lessons, together with Marie-Louise Hallo.

Miss Skelton was thirty at this time, gentle and retiring; her family disowned her when she had become a Catholic, which earned her the Catez's sympathy and support. Elizabeth enjoyed the English lessons; to her musician's ear it sounded like the language of birds.

Elizabeth was also trying to improve her handwriting. Unfortunately, she decided on a fashionable but very ornate style that was totally unsuitable for her and made her writing almost illegible. She often apologized for it in her letters. When she was a novice in Carmel, the prioress appointed Sr. Agnes, who had beautiful, classic handwriting, to give her lessons. She taught Elizabeth a more rounded, simple, and clear style that suited her character far more.

The two girls also took sewing lessons and made many of their clothes themselves. As Elizabeth herself said, she was a bit of a coquette; she also had excellent taste and was always beautifully and fashionably dressed.

Elizabeth had already established a framework for all these activities, for which the days seemed far too short. She would always try to go to the seven o'clock Mass, usually at the Good Shepherd convent nearby, now that Carmel's chapel was barred to her. Very few knew, though, that she would get up much earlier to spend some time in prayer, always on her knees.

There were worries for the family, though. On their return from holiday, Mme. Catez's health began to give them cause for concern.

She never really recovered fully from the snakebite she had suffered years earlier, and now the wound erupted again. By the beginning of December she was seriously ill, and there was the possibility that she would become a permanent invalid. Elizabeth, therefore, had to face the fact that she might have to remain at home to look after her mother and might never be able to realize her dream of entering Carmel. Her anguished prayers for the recovery of a mother whom she loved deeply and tenderly were doubly intense, then, with her own vocation at risk. By the beginning of February she was resigned to the possibility, writing, on the feast of the Purification, in the only volume of her diaries that survived:

> On each feast of Our Lady I renew my consecration to that good Mother. Today I gave myself to her, and once more threw myself into her arms. With even more complete confidence I commended my calling, my vocation to her. Since Jesus no longer wants me, may his will be done, but I will become holy in the world: may nothing stop me going to him, may the trifles of earth not preoccupy me, may I not cling to them! I am the bride of Jesus; we are so intimately united; nothing can separate us. (D 2)

This time of uncertainty about being able to enter Carmel was valuable; she was able to penetrate to the inner heart of the Carmelite life that was union with God by love, rather than pining for the externals. She realized a true Carmelite spirit was not something that could be taken away from her; she could be a genuine Carmelite wherever she was.

She threw herself into an enthusiastic round of prayer and penance, which was tempered only by her mother's disapproval. At the beginning of February, for example, she started to skip breakfast. After three days her mother found out and gave her a big scolding, as she noted in her diary, "Should I carry on? I don't think so…!" (D 6).

At the beginning of January she attended a retreat given by the Jesuits. Following their advice, she started to keep a notebook, recording all her lapses during the day. One entry notes that her hot temper was still her dominant fault:

> Today I had the joy of offering to Jesus several sacrifices
> where my dominant fault was concerned, but they cost me
> a lot! It makes me realize how weak I am. I feel that when
> I am criticized unjustly, my blood boils in my veins, and
> my whole being is in revolt!... But Jesus was with me, I
> listened to his voice deep within me, and I was ready to
> put up with anything for love of him! (D 1)

Her confessor after Abbé Sellenet left was Msgr. Golmard, whom she felt wasn't strict enough; she wanted to change to Abbé Chesnay, the Jesuit who preached the retreat. Her mother, undoubtedly fearing he might encourage Elizabeth to too much excess, made it plain she wasn't happy about the change, and Elizabeth dropped the subject.

She enthusiastically attended the extra days of prayer, of exposition of the Blessed Sacrament, run by the parish, but again, when she found her mother wasn't happy about it all, she stayed at home. It was all valuable experience, teaching her that the biggest sacrifice of self-denial was denying one's own will. It enriched her prayer. Commenting on her reading of Saint Teresa's *Way of Perfection* and her treatment of contemplative prayer, she notes:

> When she speaks of contemplation, that stage of prayer
> when God does everything and we do nothing, when he
> unites us so intimately to himself that it is no longer we
> who live, but God who lives in us, etc. Yes, I recognize in
> this description those moments of sublime rapture the
> Master often raised me to during that Retreat and even
> since then. (D 14)

Another entry in her diary gives some idea of what happened in these moments of almost ecstatic prayer, which were not ecstasies in the strict sense:

> During these divine exchanges, these sublime ecstasies, I
> beg Jesus for his Cross. That Cross is support, my hope. I
> want to share that Cross with my Master, who allows me
> to have such a wonderful share in it, choosing me for his
> confidant, for one who consoles his heart! By my love, my
> attentiveness, my sacrifices, my prayers, I want to make

him forget his sorrows. I want to love him on behalf of
those who don't love him, and I also want to bring back to
him those he loves so much! (D 8)

One of those whom she was holding specially in her prayer, offering up her communions and her sacrifices, was their elderly landlord,
M. Chapuis. He was an excellent man, wrote Elizabeth, and very charitable, but one who had no time for religion. She longed for his conversion and was hoping that a mission to be held shortly in the parish
would be the means of bringing him back to the faith.

The mission, which she had been eagerly awaiting, began on March
4, and Elizabeth attended the splendid opening ceremony in the ca-
thedral. She wasn't able to get to all of the talks and sermons; sometimes she was obliged to attend a dinner in town, or her mother frowned
on her attending too many of the mission events. Those she did attend, though, she made notes on afterward. Although she found many
of them helpful and deeply moving, there were others that disturbed
her, or that she disagreed with. As with most missions of the time, the
sermons contained a good deal of hellfire and damnation, but love
absorbed any fears that she had had as a child. She had gone far beyond the stage of being impelled to love God through fear of hell. She
wrote in her diary after a sermon on death and judgment:

> The extraordinary thing is I no longer fear God's
> judgment; this evening I haven't the least bit of dread.
> Jesus, why tremble at appearing before you? Could
> you condemn—in spite of her weakness and number-
> less faults—one who has sacrificed everything for you...?
> (D 37)

Again, when one of the preachers said they shouldn't go to dances
or the theater unless obliged to, or that it was wrong to go to Communion in the morning and go dancing in the evening, or that it was a
grave sin to give oneself up to feasts unless for a serious reason, she
wasn't totally convinced, noting that she would speak to Abbé Lion,
one of the mission fathers.

She met Abbé Lion when, as was the custom during missions, she
made a general confession. She had hoped to go to confession on that

Tuesday, but there were so many people that she had to leave it until the following day; while she was waiting, though, a friend noticed her kneeling there, motionless and totally absorbed, for an hour and a half. "She seemed surrounded by an atmosphere all her own," she said, "that separated her from all that was going on around her" (Souv. 54).

During her confession Abbé Lion was able to confirm, as had other confessors, that she had never lost her baptismal innocence, which gave her immense consolation. He was also able to tell her that he considered that she had a genuine vocation. This was reassuring, especially since a few days earlier she had noted in her diary that her mother had completely recovered from her illness, although the infection would always be latent in the wound. At last she was able to hope for Carmel once more. Abbé Lion agreed to speak to Msgr. Golmard, her confessor, on her behalf.

Things began to happen speedily. A few days later, on March 20, Guite told her she had spoken to their mother, begging her to let Elizabeth follow her vocation, since she would be happy only in Carmel. Her mother insisted she was too young, but reluctantly agreed she could if she was still of the same mind when she was twenty.

Elizabeth couldn't help weeping tears of joy, but she was sensitive enough to know that her mother and sister were silently weeping very different tears at the thought of losing her. She was not thinking only of her own concerns, though. Her prayers were with those who, she hoped, would be drawn back to God through the mission, especially M. Chapuis. That "follower of Voltaire" fell ill during the mission, which encouraged Elizabeth to redouble her prayers that his illness might be a means of grace and reconsideration for him. At first it seemed as if her prayers were being answered; just over a week later, somewhat recovered, M. Chapuis actually attended one of the mission evenings.

"Oh, may he not resist the call of God," she prayed. "Good Mother, touch his heart, convert him, I beg you" (D 115). Her prayers were all the more urgent in that there weren't many more mission days left. To her delight, her mother also acted. Mme. Catez had the courage to pay him a visit and talk to him about going to confession. "She was horribly afraid of doing more harm than good, and sending him into a rage," wrote Elizabeth in her diary, "for he is terribly sharp. By a miracle from Mary, he took it in good part and thanked mother, and told her he was very tired.... Maybe he'd do it a bit later on. Still, he was very shaken" (D 121).

Her optimism, though, proved unfounded. After Mme. Catez had prepared the way by going to see him, she went to Msgr. Golmard to ask him to send one of the missioners. Abbé Lion went, and Elizabeth was full of confidence, but M. Chapuis's response was an emphatic "no" that left no doubt about his unwillingness to be converted. He died four years later, still unrepentant, when Elizabeth was in Carmel.

On March 26 Guite again spoke to her mother about Elizabeth's vocation. Mme. Catez replied that since neither Elizabeth herself nor Msgr. Golmard had spoken to her about it, she thought Elizabeth had given up the idea. After dinner, therefore, she went to Elizabeth, who made it plain she was as determined as ever to enter Carmel. Eventually her mother agreed that if she was still of the same mind in two years time, she could enter when she was twenty-one; she couldn't in good conscience think of leaving her younger sister before then. At the back of Mme. Catez's mind, perhaps, was the thought that if her health was still bad and Elizabeth entered Carmel, it would be Guite who would have to look after her. Elizabeth wrote afterward:

> Truly, it must be Mary who has gained this grace for me, for I have never seen her like that before. When I saw the two of them crying for me, I was in a flood of tears, too! Jesus, it must be you calling me, supporting me, it must have been you holding out your arms to those I love so much, otherwise my heart would break.... My Master, I know you want me, and you are giving me strength and courage. In my tears, I feel a calm and immense sweetness. Yes, soon I'll be able to answer your call. During the next two years I'm going to redouble my efforts to be a bride less unworthy of you. (D 105)

Only five days later, however, it became clear how reluctantly Mme. Catez had given permission for Elizabeth's eventual entry into Carmel. She came home in great excitement with the news that she had received a superb offer of marriage for Elizabeth, of the sort that wouldn't come her way again. Before speaking to Elizabeth, she had gone to Msgr. Golmard, who advised her to speak to Elizabeth and point out all the advantages. He said it would be a good test of her vocation, although he couldn't pronounce on that vocation, but that Mme. Catez shouldn't do anything without speaking to Elizabeth first.

Elizabeth remained completely unmoved. "My heart is no longer free," she wrote, "I have given it to the King of kings, and it is no longer mine to give away" (D 124). The day was Good Friday, and she poured out her heart not only to her diary but also in a poem:

At the foot of your Cross, beloved,
Jesus, my crucified Love,
I come to ask you again,
Take my heart beyond return.
Heavenly Spouse, Savior divine,
I give up all happiness,
Every union here on earth,
To be yours alone.
To give you love for love. (P 69)

On Easter Sunday Elizabeth sang bittersweet alleluias. She was sad that the mission had ended, and M. Chapuis had not come back to the faith:

Alleluia, alleluia. Good Jesus, I am weeping both with glory and with joy today; weeping that the Mission is ended and weeping above all for M. Chapuis's hardness of heart. This morning I heard your voice in the depths of my heart, telling me not to despair, that if my prayers seem to have gone unheard so far, nevertheless, my intercessions and all my sufferings have done your heart good. This consoles me, but how can I rejoice when you, my Spouse, are suffering? Yet you can rejoice in seeing how many have been converted during this mission, and so I can pass this Easter Day a little less sadly. I unite myself to the joy of your heart. Think only on this lovely day of those lost sheep who have returned to the Shepherd! (D 128)

And, too, she had been given her mother's longed-for permission to enter Carmel, even though there were still two weary years to wait.

5

POSTULANT OUTSIDE THE WALLS
Parish Apostolate

April brought horrible weather, hot and unhealthily humid. A flu epidemic swept through Dijon, and Mme. Catez was one of its many victims. It left her very weak and forced her once again to rest, very trying for one who was normally so active.

Elizabeth's circle of friends was beginning to break up. At the end of April she wrote to Marie-Louise Maurel that two of her friends were marrying. One was Marie-Caroline Delagoutte, "whom I love very much and who is moving away from Dijon to marry a naval officer. We saw each other often and I'm sorry to see our lovely friendship come to an end, even while I'm rejoicing at my friend's happiness: one mustn't be selfish in one's affections!" (L 23).

For two and a half years before she entered Carmel, Elizabeth, with Guite and other friends, belonged to a parish choir run by Sr. Joseph Georges. To Elizabeth's delight the choir went to sing in the Carmelite chapel for the feast of St. Joseph. It was a precious moment of being where her heart was so often, but more was to follow very shortly. Quite unexpectedly in June, Mme. Catez lifted her ban on visits to Carmel. On June 20 Elizabeth made her first visit to the parlor since the ban and celebrated her delight in verse:

> O my Jesus, my only Love,
> My Bridegroom, my divine Friend,
> You alone know how much I love you,
> For you read my heart.
> Thank you.
> For you have heard my prayer.
> I return to my dear monastery,
> See what joy floods my heart,
> Good Master, I offer you my happiness. (P 71)

In "Carmel's poor parlor / Where everything breathes a heavenly fragrance," she once again met Mother Marie of Jesus who had been elected prioress just over three years earlier, and was now in her second term of office. At this visit Elizabeth made her formal request to enter the community.

The Dijon community that Elizabeth was asking to join had a long history going back to the very beginnings of the order in France. It had been founded in 1605 by the Venerable Mother Anne of Jesus, close friend and companion of Teresa of Avila, the third house to be opened after Paris and Pontoise.

The foundation had been established on September 21, 1605, in a small house on the Rue Charbonnerie, but this soon proved too small for the nuns, and in 1613 they moved into larger premises on the Rue Sainte-Anne. The community flourished there for nearly two hundred years until the laws of the French Revolution scattered the sisters and brought community life to an end in 1790. The buildings were eventually taken over by the Ministry of War and turned into a barracks.

It was not until the 1860s, when the papacy was going through a difficult time, that the subprioress of the Paris Carmel, Mother Marie of the Trinity, felt urged to make a vow to found a Carmel dedicated to praying for the pope and the preservation of the faith in France and Italy. At first she tried to establish a house in Strasbourg, but eventually the community was led to Dijon, where, in 1866, they set up a small house while a new monastery was being built for them on vacant ground. The foundation stone was blessed on July 25, 1868, and soon the monastery was established on Boulevard Carnot.

By the time Elizabeth asked to be admitted, it was a thriving and flourishing community, and under Mother Marie of Jesus' leadership, it was loving, united, and fervent. Indeed, the previous two or three years had seen a remarkable stream of young women seeking admittance, and the community was growing beyond its capacity to receive them.

Mother Marie of Jesus, therefore, was planning a new foundation at Paray-le-Monial, where years before St. Margaret Mary Alacoque had received her visions of the Sacred Heart. In the meantime she was gathering her band of aspirants whom she called her "postulants outside the walls," and training them in the Carmelite spirit until the new foundation would be ready to receive them.

In the parlor she encouraged Elizabeth to speak of her way of prayer and found it to be simple and integrated. The Master was there within her, forming her to his plan. Elizabeth complained of doing nothing, taken out of herself by him who was doing everything.

There was an immediate rapport between prioress and postulant; they were kindred spirits in their generosity of soul and the wideness of their love. Marie of Jesus, long experienced in guiding young people in the love of God, recognized in Elizabeth someone who was exceptionally gifted in prayer and marked her out as one who would be destined not for the Dijon Carmel but for the new foundation at Paray-le-Monial.

Elizabeth had little time to enjoy her new freedom to visit Carmel, for the family was soon off on their summer vacations. They went first to the Jura, where they immersed themselves in the peace of the countryside, and Mme. Catez could recuperate after her illness. In a letter to Marie-Louise Maurel, Elizabeth called it her Thebaid, after the solitude of the desert fathers:

> We are in the country in a pine forest, in a true little Thebaid, and we are spending all our time out of doors: it's so good among the trees! We take books and work and don't go back in until the evening in time for dinner. I wish you could share my solitude, for we are living just like hermits. In spite of that I'm not bored for a moment, it's so good to live quietly in the country. The good air of the Jura and the rest has done mother a world of good, she really needed it, for she was very tired when we left Dijon, and you can imagine how pleased I am to see her looking so much better! (L 24)

It was to be her last visit to the Jura. On August 17 they traveled on to Switzerland where they stayed for three weeks, and then returned to France and the Vosges, where they stayed at Mirecourt with Mme. Hougue, an aunt of theirs.

Unlike previous years, though, she couldn't wait to return to Dijon. Now she had her visits to Carmel to look forward to. She soon made a new circle of friends from among the "postulants outside the walls." There were Marguerite Gallot, who never actually entered in the end, and Marthe Weishardt, who entered Carmel in 1895 but did not persevere, although she remained in close contact with the community. In the circle of friends she was known by the name she would have in religion, Marie-Thérèse.

Another friend, Marie Bouveret, introduced Elizabeth to a wider field of activity. Marie persuaded her to help with running a youth club for the children of workers at a tobacco factory in the Boulevard Voltaire, and they also helped with catechism classes in St. Peter's parish. The two of them would arrange to meet in the Carmelite chapel and would then go and visit families whose children hadn't made their First Communion.

Elizabeth had always had the gift of attracting younger children. Françoise de Sourdon, for example, eight years her junior, doted on her, and she found that the less privileged children in her catechism class and the youth club fell equally under her spell. She had the ability to make the Christian life attractive. Her own love for God was so obvious in everything about her that young children, as well as her friends and acquaintances, were drawn to long for a similar experience for themselves. She had an exceptionally well-rounded personality. Her deep prayer life enveloped her in quiet strength and self-control, yet at the same time she had tremendous drive and was full of life and fun.

She found she was as gifted at storytelling as her grandfather had been; she made up plays for the children to perform and devised games for them that they could enjoy, yet at the same time introduced them to the Christian faith. So popular did she become that she had to conceal her address from them; otherwise, they would have come around for her at all hours.

It was probably on her return from the summer holidays and with her renewed contact with Carmel that she obtained a copy of the autobiography of St. Thérèse of Lisieux. Thérèse of the Child Jesus and of the Holy Face was a young Carmelite who had died two years earlier on September 30, 1897. No doubt Elizabeth was envious that Thérèse had been allowed to enter Carmel at the unusually early age of fifteen; she had died of tuberculosis after an outwardly uneventful life at the age of twenty-four.

Her prioress, Mother Agnes, who was also her sister, discerned her unassuming holiness, though, and toward the end of Thérèse's life ordered her to write an account of her life and spirituality, which Thérèse called her "Little Way," the way of spiritual childhood.

On the occasion of a nun's death, it is the custom for a Carmel to send other Carmels a circular, a short account of the deceased sister's life. On Thérèse's death the Lisieux Carmel made the unusual decision of sending out copies of her autobiography, and it was published for general circulation a year later. So popular was it that the first edition of 2,000 copies was sold out within six months.

It was not long before Thérèse's influence was showing itself in Elizabeth's writings and in her letters to her friends. Not that her spirituality was changed in any great way, for the two young women were very much one in the simplicity of their love for God, which impelled them to express their sacrificial love not in extraordinary deeds but by using the circumstances of their daily lives. Rather, Thérèse extended the ways in which Elizabeth could express her spiritual life.

On June 9, 1895, the feast of the Holy Trinity, Thérèse had made an offering of herself to God's merciful love, expressed in a prayer she kept with her for the rest of her life:

> O my God! Most Blessed Trinity, I desire to *Love* You and make You *Loved*, to work for the glory of Holy Church....
> I desire, in a word, to be a saint, but feel my helplessness and I beg you, O my God! to be Yourself my *Sanctity*!
> ...In the evening of this life, I shall appear before You with empty hands, for I do not ask You, Lord, to count my works. All our justice is stained in Your eyes. I wish, then, to be clothed in Your own *Justice* and to receive from Your *Love* the eternal possession of *Yourself*. I want no other *throne*, no other *crown* but You, my Beloved! (SOS, Act of Oblation, p. 276)

Toward the end of November Elizabeth wrote her own act of offering that is permeated by Thérèse's influence:

> Make me a martyr of your love, that I may die of that martyrdom. Take from me the freedom to displease you, that I may never cause you the least pain. Crush, tear out of my heart all that displeases you in it. I want always to do your will, to respond always to your grace. My Master, I want to be a saint for your sake, be you my sanctity, for I know my weakness. Jesus, thank you for all the graces you have given me, thank you, above all, for testing me. It is so good to suffer for you, with you. May my every heartbeat be a cry of gratitude and love. (NI 4)

Thérèse's style tended to be somewhat flowery and sentimental, which could sometimes disguise the solid theological sense of her spirituality and the uncompromising and radical self-giving to God that was the basis of her "Little Way." Elizabeth's style was far starker, but she went unerringly to the heart of Thérèse's spirituality, making her own those words and phrases that best expressed her inner life. She is not aping her older sister but is using the words because they are a precise expression of her own experience of God.

At the end of November she wrote to Marie-Louise Maurel to congratulate her on her engagement to Joseph Ambry, a grocer from Carcassonne. She was happy for Marie-Louise, but more than content, too, that the Master had chosen a different path for her.

She was attending a retreat at the time given by the new Bishop of Dijon, Msgr. Le Nordez, who had been appointed the previous July and would take up his position officially the following February. He soon became a close friend of the family.

In January Mme. Catez fell on some stairs while going to Mass and injured her back. Fortunately she didn't break any bones, although she was badly bruised and was bedridden for a short while. At the end of January, Elizabeth attended another retreat given by the Jesuit fathers and was able to satisfy to some degree her hunger for prayer. In her diary she said she wanted "to live within, in that cell you have made in my heart, where I see you, where I experience you so well" (D 140).

She was able to go to confession once more to Abbé Chesnay, because she wanted firmer direction, holy as her regular confessor, Abbé Golmard, was. At the end of the retreat Elizabeth went to see "Our Mother," as she called Mother Marie of Jesus according to Carmelite custom, grateful that she now had her guidance in prayer to rely on, too.

Elizabeth summed up the grace of the retreat in a lovely prayer that epitomizes her spiritual life and remained remarkably consistent throughout her life. The Thérèsian influence is there, but it is unmistakably Elizabeth's own:

> Jesus, my Beloved, how wonderful it is to love you, to belong to you, to have you for my only All! Now that you are coming every day to me, may our union be even closer. May my life be a continual prayer, a long act of love. May nothing whatever distract me from you, no noise or distractions. I would so love, my Master, to live with you in silence. But what I love most of all is to do your will, and since you want me to be in the world at present, I submit myself with all my heart for love of you. I offer you the cell of my heart to be your little Bethany; come and live there, I love you so much.... I would like to console you and I offer myself to you as a victim, Master, for you, with you. I accept in advance every sacrifice, every trial, even that of no longer feeling you with me. I only ask one thing: always to be generous and faithful, always; I never want to take it back. I want to do your will perfectly, to respond always to your grace; I long to be a saint with you and for you, but I realize my weakness— be you my sanctity. If I ever take it back, I beg you, I plead with you: while I am yours take me, let me die. I am your 'little spoiled pet,' you tell me, but soon perhaps trials will come and then it will be me who will give to you. Master, it isn't the gifts, the consolations you pour out on me that I'm looking for, it is you and you alone! Watch over me always, make me more and more your own, may everything in me belong to you: break, cut away, all that displeases you that I may be all yours. Each heartbeat of mine is an act of love. My Jesus, my God, how good it is to love you, to be totally yours! (NI 5)

"May Elizabeth disappear, and only Jesus remain," she added in her diary (NI 6). This prayer was especially impassioned because in her diary on January 27, she noted that her great friend Marie-Louise Hallo was leaving in five days' time to enter the novitiate of the Sacred Heart Sisters at Conflans. It was hard for Elizabeth to see her friend follow her heart when, as yet, she could not. "Like her, I would like to be able to say farewell to those I love so dearly, and to leave everything for you, too. But my hour has not yet come, may your will be done. May your holy will, my God, always be my own!" (D 156).

She longed for the physical solitude of Carmel, but as she could not yet have it, she asked God to give her the solitude of the heart that could be with her wherever she was. Although she never showed it, and only the most perceptive discerned it, the social round of balls and soireés of the winter season were irksome to her when her heart was pulled in such a different direction:

> You know, my good Master, that my consolation when I go to these reunions, these celebrations, my consolation is to recollect myself and rejoice in your presence, for I feel you so much within me, my supreme Good. At these reunions where no one is thinking of you, it seems to me that you are happy that there is one heart, even one so poor and feeble as mine, that does not forget you! (D 138)

Although she had rejected one suitor, there were many who hoped to be more successful, attracted by her radiance, her vivacity, and quiet dignity. One of these was her childhood friend, Charles Hallo, fast growing into manhood; even Msgr. Brunhes, the Bishop of Montpellier, once boasted that he had danced with Elizabeth of Dijon. But Berthe de Massiac, one of Elizabeth's friends, overheard some young men at a dance say, as they looked over the assembly of young ladies with an eye to marriage: "She's not for us, look at her expression" (LLL 9).

6

INDWELLING OF THE TRINITY
Deepening Prayer Life

Elizabeth's visits to Carmel continued, and she became great friends
with the extern sisters, helping them with the cleaning and dusting
and looking after the chapel and external parts of the monastery. They
long remembered the energy with which she dusted and polished,
while at the same time being absorbed in God. They were experienced in assessing the quality of the many hopeful young women
who came to the monastery and already recognized some exceptional
qualities in Elizabeth.

During one of her visits with Mother Marie of Jesus, Elizabeth
was given the name she would have in Carmel, Marie Elizabeth of the
Trinity—although the "Marie" was rarely used. She was disappointed;
she had set her heart on being called Elizabeth of Jesus. However,
since that was what her prioress had decided, she made no objections
and hid her disappointment. The choice, although she didn't realize it
at the time, was to be prophetic, and it was not long before she recognized its significance. In June, after the family had returned to Dijon
from a pilgrimage to Paray-le-Monial organized by the Jesuits, Elizabeth was introduced to Abbé Vallée, the prior of the Dominicans in
Dijon, who was giving a retreat to the community. His teaching was
to have an enduring influence on her, and her letters soon started to
bear the imprint of his rich doctrinal spirituality. He was also able to
throw light on the development of her prayer life.

The diary notes she had made during the mission the previous
year showed that the talks on prayer and meditation emphasized vo-
cal and petitionary prayer; Abbé Lion's talk on meditation described
prayer according to the Ignatian method, which Elizabeth noted in
her diary:

> Before meditation, recollect oneself; then read slowly
> savoring every word, letting them sink into the soul; read
> over again those passages that strike one the most but
> never read from curiosity.
> Make a resolution, this is very important, for medita-
> tion without a resolution is three-quarters wasted ...then,
> never give up prayer. Give even two minutes to it if there
> isn't time for more. (D 86)

Elizabeth noted that she wanted to discuss the subject with Abbé Lion when she next went to confession to him; she was obviously troubled that her own prayer didn't fit this picture at all. In her prayer she put herself straight away in the presence of God, although by now she habitually lived there anyway. It was not so much what Elizabeth herself did in prayer, but what God himself was doing in her; she simply had to be there with him.

She rarely used books during prayer, although she did read at other times; she was studying Teresa of Avila's writings around this time. But throughout her life she read very little, although what she did read was fully in accord with Abbé Lion's advice; when some idea or thought or phrase from her favorite writers struck her, she made it totally her own. She used it because it precisely reflected her own inner life and understanding.

It was clear from her diary notes afterward, though, that Abbé Lion didn't really have a true understanding of this. He told her that when she was strong enough to go without consolations, she would have dry and arid periods when it would seem as if Jesus had withdrawn himself. This was perfectly sound, but he obviously believed that Elizabeth's almost effortless absorption in prayer was based on "consolations," the type of emotional fervor and ease of prayer that God often gives at the beginning of the spiritual life but eventually gives way to dryness and a sense that God is no longer there.

He was therefore giving Elizabeth a gentle warning that her former prayer wouldn't last, and she had to be prepared for dryness and arid-ity when she was "strong enough" to bear it. But she had already passed beyond that stage. Her facility in prayer was a genuine gift of contemplative prayer and not a beginner's fervor. She did indeed have periods of dryness when prayer was an effort, but her generosity of spirit was already well honed by her habitual self-denial and self-forgetfulness.

And in the period leading up to her meeting with Abbé Vallée, she had been aware of a further development that she was at a loss to explain. She was practiced in keeping herself in the presence of God, of being aware that God was with her, but now she sensed a presence within her, as if she was being "dwelt in." What did it mean? It meant, said Abbé Vallée, that she really was dwelt in. After explaining how God is in us by his essence, power, and presence, he went on to quote 1 Corinthians 3:16: "Do you not know that you are the temple of God and that the Holy Spirit dwells in you?" He showed how, by the grace of baptism, we become that spiritual temple, and the Holy Spirit with the Father and the Son, who are inseparable, come and make their dwelling within us. There, in that inner temple, the Trinity can receive the interior praise and worship that are due to God.

This somewhat dry doctrinal explanation drew her powerfully and irresistibly within to experience the reality of what Abbé Vallée was describing even as he spoke. He realized she was no longer listening; Elizabeth later said she was now longing for him to be silent.

Abbé Vallée was deeply impressed with her: "It was a real joy to speak of Our Lord and his grace within us," he said, "to one who was so pure, intuitive, and also so simple, and whose will as well as intellect was given to her Master from her earliest years" (Souv. 66–67).

Once again for a short while she had to leave Dijon and all that was happening for the annual round of visits. The previous year she made her final visit to the Jura; now she was to take her final leave of friends and relatives in the Midi. She had intended to travel to Paris with Guite for Marie-Louise Hallo's clothing ceremony on June 24, but this was postponed until September or October because Marie-Louise's health was giving cause for concern. They therefore planned to set off for the Midi the first week in July, stopping first at Tarbes to see the Rostangs, then on to Biarritz and Lourdes before traveling to Carlipa.

While at Tarbes Elizabeth visited the Carmel there and spoke to the prioress, who later said that during the quite long visit, she had to call the extern sister to the parlor. The sister afterward asked her if she knew Elizabeth was on her knees, and must have been kneeling for the whole time.

Elizabeth made another visit to the parlor, this time with her mother, to see a young sister who had just received the veil. She couldn't help her tears flowing at the sight of the young Carmelite's joy, and her mother realized just how much Carmel meant to her daughter. "Don't cry," she said as they left the parlor, "I won't make you wait much longer" (Souv. 63–64).

At Biarritz they had their first glimpse of the Atlantic Ocean, and Elizabeth was enthralled. "It's wonderful, and I can't tell you what a superb sight it is," she wrote to Marie-Louise Maurel. "I love that boundless, limitless horizon! Mother and Guite couldn't drag me away from my contemplation of it, and I think they found me somewhat tiresome; I'm sure you would understand though" (L 30).

They spent just one day in Biarritz and two days in Lourdes, where Elizabeth was able to receive Communion in the grotto. Then they went on to Carlipa to the usual warm welcome from their aunts. They were almost as upset as Mme. Catez to think of Elizabeth entering Carmel and, no doubt to her mother's gratification, did their best to put her off. She still dressed with her usual elegance and carefully arranged hair. (Perhaps her one lapse in fashion sense was captured in a photograph taken in the spring of the previous year, in which Elizabeth was wearing a hat with a truly amazing concoction of tulle erupting from it.)

"For a future Carmelite, we think you could be more simple," her aunts remarked, and Elizabeth replied with a wide smile, "that before entering Carmel, St. Teresa acted the same way, and she wanted to imitate her in everything." And when a priest felt that the Carmelite way of life might prove too austere for her, she just shrugged, "Oh well, then I'll die" (RB 13:4; LLL 9–10).

They stayed in Carlipa until the beginning of September, when they went on to Limoux and then to Saint-Hilaire for a week, where they stayed with Mme. Lignon and were able to see Canon Angles and his sister once more. There was a full round of entertainments for the family too, a visit to the Château Chesnel, musical evenings, and dances.

Some sixty years later, one of those present, a Mlle. Auburtin, could still recall those musical evenings and the impression Elizabeth had made on her as she played the piano for them: "Elizabeth had a rare and delightful talent as a pianist; she felt music deeply," knowing how to express what she felt. "It seems to me that I can still hear her playing 'Le chant du nautonier.'" She added that Elizabeth was "very lively and endowed with great charm.... She enthusiastically took part in the diversions of our age" (LLL 60). Mlle Auburtin added, "Those days I spent with her have left me, after all these years, with a vivid memory of her. Elizabeth was too attractive to allow us to forget her."

Mlle. Auburtin noted that there was not a trace of austerity about her; a basic element of Elizabeth's austerity, her unobtrusive self-denial, was to subordinate her own urgent inclinations to silence, solitude, and prayer to the obligations her present life and its social commitments made on her. But she had for a long time learned how to be silent and at prayer in that precious cell within herself where her Master dwelt, whatever the external distractions.

Although she took a spirited part in all the entertainments put on for them, Elizabeth later wrote to her mother from Carmel that "while I was dancing with the others and playing quadrilles downstairs in the large drawing room, I was haunted by Carmel" (L 178). A photograph taken of her at this time shows some of the strain this longing inevitably caused. Her hands are clenched awkwardly, her face is tense and serious, even allowing for the immobility demanded by photography at that time. Her mother's face, too, shows the strain, and she looks like a woman far older than her fifty-three years.

They stopped in Paris on their way back to Dijon, and Elizabeth visited Montmartre and the Carmelite church of Our Lady of Victories; they toured the Paris Exhibition, too, which she found interesting, although she detested the crowds and the noise. Guite teased her that she had the air of someone returning from the Congo. She was glad to be back in Dijon once more at the beginning of October.

She found Marie-Louise Hallo there, too. Her health had continued to be a concern, and she had returned home for the present, much to her mother's delight. If her health improved, she might try the convent again, but for the moment Elizabeth could have her companionship for the winter, at least. No doubt Mme. Catez was also happy to see Marie-Louise back; it raised the possibility that even if Elizabeth were to enter Carmel, she also might leave after a while.

Marie-Louise was well enough to help Elizabeth with her children's club at the tobacco factory. The children had given Elizabeth a rapturous welcome on her return, and she went to their awards ceremony, touched by their obvious pleasure in having her back.

She was also in touch once again with her beloved Carmel. She got bronchitis, but this didn't prevent her and Marie-Louise from helping out with the dusting and polishing of the chapel and arranging the flowers in preparation for the feast of St. Teresa.

The following month she went to the clothing ceremony of Marie-Antoinette Rollet, who took the name of Marie-Angèle of the Infant Jesus and the Precious Blood. She was allowed to escort the young novice to the cloister door, and Mother Marie of Jesus made the sign of the cross over her. "Then the door closed...without me!" she wrote to Canon Angles shortly afterward, describing the ceremony. "I can assure you my heart was really heavy. I offered to Jesus the tears that couldn't help falling and surrendered myself to his will, for his will is best" (L 38).

In the same letter she mentioned that she had gone with her mother to see the bishop, Msgr. Le Nordez, about her entry into Carmel, and the bishop did his best to help Mme. Catez in her distress. As she explained to Canon Angles, it was a difficult time for both of them:

> If you knew how much I suffer in seeing my poor mother so distraught as my twenty-first birthday approaches.... She is so changeable: one day she tells me one thing, the next day it's something else. On the feast of All Souls she seemed to be perfectly agreeable to my entering and even told me I could enter in the summer. I had prayed so hard to my poor father to inspire her! Yet two days later she completely changed her mind! Abbé

Golmard has told me to promise her nothing, so if
she asks me to wait I haven't committed myself to
anything; pray for me please. It is hard to make those
you love suffer, but it is for him! If he wasn't giving me
the strength, sometimes I wonder what would happen
to me, but he is with me and with him one can do everything. (L 38)

It was desperately hard for all of them. They were a very close-
knit family, and Elizabeth adored her mother; it was hard, then, that
in following the call of her Master, she had to hurt those she loved
most. As she remarked to Marie-Louise Maurel, her greatest suffering was to see them suffer.

By now she was using the name she would have in religion when
writing to Marguerite Gallot, Berthe Tardy, and others of her friends
in the group of aspirants, and putting JM+JT (for Jesus, Mary, Joseph, and Teresa) in the Carmelite way at the top of her letters—
anything to bring the reality nearer.

Easter was early in 1901, and visits to the parlor ceased during
Lent. She was meeting her friends at the Carmel, though, and helping
the extern sisters with all the many preparations during Holy Week
and Easter. On Holy Thursday night she kept vigil for three hours,
and a short prayer she wrote that day gives some idea of her thoughts:

I suffer, my God. But I want to remain that way for as
long as you wish, because you want to unite yourself more closely to me and this blessed suffering purifies me. Give me as much as you wish, then, but help
me, I am so weak. You well know that it is you and
you alone that I love, you alone I cling to! Love, it is
good to be able to give to you, who have spoiled me so
much. (NI 11)

She was there again for the Good Friday ceremonies and spent the
day with Berthe Tardy. Berthe was thirty-one at this time, a little older
than most of the others. Family commitments prevented her from entering Carmel for the present, but she was to become the major bene-
factress of the Paray-le-Monial foundation, placing an inheritance she
received at their disposal and eventually entering there.

This foundation had received a temporary setback because of the troubled religious situation in France at that time. The previous November, Cardinal Perraud had refused permission for the foundation because the socialist coalition government's anticlerical campaign put religious orders in a precarious situation. The Law of Associations was shortly to be passed that put severe restrictions on religious orders and their institutions and even caused them to be persecuted and hounded out of France. Many religious were already leaving the country, and it seemed foolhardy that Mother Marie of Jesus should think of founding a new monastery when so many were being forcibly closed.

She remained peacefully confident, though, and spent the whole of that Lent in intense prayer and almost complete solitude. By Easter the cardinal was very much more in favor and on May 19, 1901, gave his authorization for the foundation. By May 24 the bishops of the relevant dioceses had also given their consent and all was set for Mother Marie of Jesus to find a house for the new Carmel.

The week after Easter Mme. Catez and Guite went to the Midi for a family wedding; with her entry into Carmel so near, Elizabeth stayed behind in Dijon with the Hallos. The weather was very bad with heavy rain and gales, but Elizabeth and Marie-Louise were delighted to have each other's company. Since the weather prevented them from going out much, they spent their time renovating their outfits for the summer and making hats for themselves after the latest Paris fashions. After dinner one evening, Charles gave them a concert of extracts from *The Barber of Seville*.

Elizabeth was also preparing a young girl for her First Communion on May 5. Louise Demoulin came from a very antireligious family and only after the death of her father when she was fourteen was she able to be baptized. She then started to attend the catechism classes at St. Peter's, but the other children, who were much younger, made fun of her. The parish priest, therefore, asked Elizabeth to give her instruction privately. Louise said later:

> Her angelic face captivated me straight away, and my affection and respect for her grew every time I met her. Her

patience and gentleness with me were boundless. And the
love with which she spoke of the great sacrament I was to
receive! She encouraged me to pray to Our Lady, sowing
the seeds of my devotion to her. I remember so well the
way she prayed with me and for me, especially during the
retreat beforehand. I was struck by her prayerfulness as we
went to the church together. Now I realize this was because she knew she was the tabernacle of Jesus. She told
me this was about to happen for me. (Souv. 55)

With her entry into Carmel drawing so near, the waiting was hard
to bear, especially with her mother and sister dreading it so much.
Marguerite Gallot, one of the friends she made at Carmel, now became one of her closest confidants, sharing her aspirations and her
anguish. Elizabeth wrote to Marguerite:

It's good to suffer, isn't it, to give something to the one
you love. I've never understood that so well until now. It
is here, at the foot of the Cross, that we realize we are his
brides; all the darkness and the suffering purifies us, sets
us free to belong wholly to him who is our All. How does
that happen? God in me and I in him, let that be our motto.
That presence of God in the hidden sanctuary within us is
so good. We find him there always, even when we don't
feel him present, for he is there all the same, perhaps even
closer then, as you say. I love to search for him there. Let
us never leave him alone, that our lives may be a continual
prayer. (L 47)

Elizabeth had said that often there seemed to be just the thinnest
of veils separating her from the vision of God. Now, though, borrowing a phrase from Thérèse of Lisieux, she said that this veil had become a solid brick wall that hid him from her. "It's very hard, isn't it,
after he has seemed so close, but I'm willing to stay like this for as
long as the Beloved wishes, for faith tells me he is there all the same;
and what are sweetness and consolations, after all? They aren't him.
And it is he alone we are looking for, isn't it?" (L 53).
    Her health was suffering, too, and with her thirst for suffering she
accepted it with joy. Fortunately, though, Mother Marie of Jesus, with

her robust common sense, was there to rein in her excesses. When she realized that some of Elizabeth's ill-health was of her own choosing, she soon put a stop to it. The previous October, for example, when Elizabeth had gotten bronchitis, the prioress had told her to pray for it to clear up. Elizabeth meekly obeyed: "Our Mother has told me to. I have no desire to be cured, it's so good to suffer for the Beloved, so I'm making this prayer under obedience" (NI 9).

Furthermore, when Mother Marie discovered Elizabeth had been suffering from severe headaches for two years from a desire to share her Master's crown of thorns, she promptly told her to pray for them to stop, which they did. Her delighted and secret possession of a hairshirt, which was making her ill from lack of sleep, was short-lived, too, once Mother Marie of Jesus found out about it.

Now, due to her long hours of kneeling in prayer, she developed synovitis of the knee. The doctor prescribed absolute rest for a couple of weeks, which prevented her from going to Mass and to Carmel and from attending the Corpus Christi procession there. By June 14, though, she was well enough to walk to Carmel, and she was busy making a dress for Guite to wear on holiday. Françoise de Sourdon—Framboise—came for a final visit, and they played duets on the piano together.

Mlle. Lalande, a friend of her mother's, came to say good-bye; she demanded to visit Carmel and speak to the prioress and, much to Elizabeth's distress, was frightened to death by the sight of the formidable grilles in the parlor.

Toward the end of June they attended a horse show in Dijon Park, the young women in their graceful summer dresses and wide, flowered hats. She wrote several chatty letters to Framboise, who was becoming very upset at her immanent departure for Carmel, assuring her of her enduring affection and giving her snippets of news: "Do you remember Cauvel, that accessory shop in Paris? One of his daughters, who married the brothers' cook a few days ago, lives here now; her husband, the famous cook, is dreadfully fat; poor boy, it's sad at his age!" (L 66). The household was also in upheaval, as they were moving from their second floor apartment to the ground floor.

In the meantime, with permission for the new foundation secured, Mother Marie of Jesus set off on June 12 with her subprioress to look at a possible site for the new convent. The parish priest in Paray-le-Monial, Abbé Gauthey, had been looking for something for them and had found a small farm and rambling old mansion near the Poor Clares that he thought might be suitable. When the two Carmelites inspected it, however, they found it totally inappropriate. The house was almost derelict, very inaccessible, and totally impractical. Abbé Gauthey obviously had an idealistic and exalted conception of the length to which Carmelite austerity could go.

They had no choice, then, but to return to Dijon, but very soon they were told of another property in the Ruelle du Loup. It was on the point of being let to the Freemasons as a lodge, and their advisers there decided to act immediately and put in an offer straightaway. Mother Marie of Jesus returned to Paray-le-Monial on June 23 with Mlle. Tardy, who was to provide most of the necessary funds, and the following day they went to inspect the property, which was a short way outside the town.

Mother Marie of Jesus was dismayed; it was a single-storied, chalet-type house with only seven or eight rooms and, she remarked, could easily fit into the choir at Dijon with room to spare. How could she expect her daughters to follow the religious life in such cramped conditions? Then she remembered the Lord's remark to Teresa of Avila when Teresa was faced with a similarly impossible property: "Do the best you can." Mother Marie made up her mind, and they returned to the town to sign the contract.

They then came back to Dijon, where packing had already begun and boxes and trunks were being stacked in the passages ready for the journey. On the way back both Mother Marie of Jesus and Mlle. Tardy, who was to enter at Paray-le-Monial as soon as the foundation had been made, had been having anguished second thoughts about the property; seeing these preparations made them realize how much of a reality the new venture was. But in spite of her reservations the prioress also had a sense, swiftly proved correct, that the foundation must be made with the greatest urgency, and decided on June 28, feast of St. Peter and St. Paul, as the date.

She therefore set off with four other sisters and on June 30 took possession of the new site. It was just in time. The following day, July 1, the Law of Associations was passed, banning the foundation of any religious houses.

The early days of the new Carmel, until a new house was built, demanded a great deal from the nuns. All their available funds had been spent in buying the property, so they were desperately poor. Fortunately the other religious communities in Paray generously provided much of their food, but they never knew where their next meal was coming from. They had so little space that workrooms had to double as cells for the sisters, with five or six of them sleeping in the partitioned garrets directly under the roof. The sleeping rooms were stiflingly hot in summer and freezing cold in winter. In these cramped conditions it was difficult to maintain the normal routine of community life and worship, but they did so with enormous love, joy, and sacrifice.

Elizabeth was soon set to go to this foundation. She undoubtedly would have put all her own considerable resources of courage, self-sacrifice, and joy into living the Carmelite life as it was being forged at Paray, but her genius for contemplative prayer needed the spacious silence, the established routine of prayer and work and worship that was available in Dijon. Besides, she loved the Dijon community dearly, and it was where her heart was. However, at this point it was not an option for her. It was adding to her mother's anguish, too. If Elizabeth were to be just around the corner in Dijon, the separation would be just that little bit less severe than if she were faraway in Paray.

The same day the foundation was made in Paray, on the night of June 30, a cyclone hit Dijon. Guite and their maid, Claire, ran round trying to close all the windows. They had to leave some of them open, though, because of the ferocity of the hailstones. Elizabeth wrote to Framboise:

> I was trapped in my room; there was a horrible rattle of broken window panes in the kitchen and my mother's room with broken glass everywhere, even behind the bed. Mother cried and thought her wardrobe was going to be

smashed. Within the space of ten minutes there was terrible damage all through Dijon. The Mere-de-Dieu is in
ruins, nothing left, and everywhere you go there's storm
damage. The Little Sisters had 10,000 francs of panes broken. At Carmel all the cloister windows were broken,
about 3,000 to 4,000 francs worth. And apart from all that,
you can't imagine how frightening it was! (L 67)

Elizabeth's twenty-first birthday was now less than three weeks
away, and still no date had been fixed for her entry into Carmel. Seeing how the uncertainty was affecting her daughter's health, Mme.
Catez courageously put her own grief aside and went to the Carmel
and asked them to fix a date as soon as possible. And so, quite suddenly, on July 19, the day after her birthday, it was all settled; Elizabeth was to travel to Paray on August 1 and enter after Mass the
following day.

She immediately began writing farewell letters to her friends and
relatives, sending them little mementos. There were last photographs
of her to be taken. Her bags were packed and sent to Paray. Even so,
their next-door neighbor, Mme. Farrat, recalled that only a few days
before she was due to leave, Elizabeth, in an effort to keep an air of
normality, bought herself a pair of gloves for her last outing.

Mme. Catez was still deeply troubled at the thought of her entering at Paray. In addition to the distance that would separate them, she
was now even more worried that the privations and hardships of the
Carmelite community would seriously undermine her daughter's
health. After speaking to a friend who urged her to seek advice from
some competent authority, she wrote to Mother Marie of Jesus. The
prioress wrote back immediately to Elizabeth herself:

You are no doubt aware that your mother and Marguerite
have asked to let you stay in Dijon; it seems that this is
also what you would prefer. I see in all this the will
of the good God which we should love and do without a
second thought. Give yourself to the Lord wherever he
wills; I don't want you here if it isn't what he wants. So I
shall receive you for Dijon, my dear child; bring
all that you have of heart and soul to love our Lord.

> I would have loved to be there to offer you to him,
> but I will not be able to, as business is keeping me here;
> but my prayer and my heart will be there to bless
> you. (Souv. 75)

It was only then that Elizabeth felt free to confide to her sister how much of a sacrifice it would have been for her to go to Paray, and that it was only the thought of making an even greater sacrifice that had made her keep silent. Guite described the last night her sister spent with them as truly dreadful and one they would never forget. Elizabeth spent it in prayer. Her mother came to her and their tears mingled. "But why do you want to leave me, then?" her mother pleaded as she saw her daughter's anguish.

"Darling mother, how can I resist the voice of God calling me? He is holding out his arms to me, telling me he is despised, scorned, forsaken. Shall I abandon him as well? He wants my sacrifice. I have to go however much it hurts me to leave you and cause you such heartbreak. I have to answer his call" (Souv. 76).

Her Rolland aunts had accused her of being heartless, but this was very far from the truth. Knowing how much pain she was causing her mother and sister nearly broke her heart, and she had the courage to go on only because she was convinced it was what God wanted of her. And it was only by doing God's will that good could come; perhaps even her loved ones might one day be reconciled to her vocation.

Two years previously, Elizabeth had written in her diary:

> Soon I will answer your call, soon I will be all yours, soon
> I will have said farewell to all that I love. The sacrifice is
> already made, my heart is set free from all things; that
> costs me little when it is for you. But there is one sacrifice
> that will be deeply painful for me and for which I beg your
> help: it is my mother and my sister. I am happy to give this
> sacrifice to you, to really have something to offer you, for
> you have overwhelmed me with gifts and what have I
> brought to you? So very little and even that little is your
> gift. At least I give you a heart that loves you, a heart that
> longs to share your suffering, that lives only for you, that

wants only you.... I will be your bride, a poor and humble
Carmelite, crucified like you, my King, my Life, my only
Love. (D 133)

That day had arrived at last. Before she left the house, Elizabeth went
to a portrait of her father and prayed for his blessing on her, and then
the family made the short journey round the corner to the Carmel.
One day she had told a friend how much she longed for suffering
and even death. "Don't delude yourself, Elizabeth," the friend replied.
"God takes people like yourself at their word and accepts their self-
giving. When you enter Carmel don't have any illusions, you will
suffer a lot. I don't know what God has in store for you; perhaps the
sufferings will be of all kinds as you want to be like your Jesus and
that is a bottomless abyss" (Souv. 71–72).

"I'm ready to take the plunge," replied Elizabeth with her generous and gentle smile. "I hope I do suffer; that's what I'm entering
Carmel for and if the good God overlooked me for a single day, I
would think he had forgotten me" (Souv. 72).

With such total self-giving the anguish within her heart was overwhelmed by an even deeper peace as they heard Mass together and
gathered in the parlor for the last farewells. The friend was there, too,
and at one point she turned round and their glances met.

"I can't describe what I saw," she said. "Her looks were almost
angelic, no longer human. Her eyes were luminous, transparent; they
shone with a heavenly light.... I'll never forget the impression she
made on me. That was the last time I saw her this side of Carmel's
grilles" (Souv. 73).

PART TWO
Her Life in Carmel

7

BRING ALL YOU HAVE OF HEART AND SOUL
Entry into Carmel

Elizabeth was received at the enclosure door by the subprioress, Mother Germaine of Jesus; behind her stretched two long lines of sisters, their veils down. Elizabeth knelt to kiss the large crucifix held out to her and then, as the heavy doors closed on the outside world, the sisters threw back their veils to reveal faces smiling in welcome. She embraced each one, and then Mother Germaine took her to the choir where she knelt and offered herself with, as Mother Marie of Jesus had expressed it, "all she had of heart and soul to love our Lord."

She was then taken to her cell to change into her postulant's clothes: a long brown dress, a short cape, and a net bonnet with wide ribbons and a net veil attached.

Shortly afterward she was joined there by Sr. Marie of the Trinity, a professed sister who was to be her "angel," a sister who would guide her through her first bewildering days in Carmel and introduce her to the rules and customs of her new life. By the time the bell rang for dinner, she had already mastered some of them: to refer to everything as "our" rather than "my" in the Carmelite way, and to tuck her hands under the short cape, as she would keep them hidden under the scapular later on.

That first community act set the pattern of her future as a Carmelite. As soon as she had finished her meal, she folded her hands under her cape, closed her eyes, and sat quietly, obviously deeply absorbed in prayer. "It's too good to last," thought the young sister who was serving, "Nobody is so mortified on the first day" (Souv. 83).

Some of the older sisters also shared her skepticism and decided to reserve judgment. Even so, when a sister sent a photograph of the community to Mother Agnes of Jesus at the Lisieux Carmel three days later, she noted in her cover letter that the group included a postulant of three days "who will become a saint for she already has a remarkable disposition for it" (LLL 68).

As her first day in Carmel drew to a close, Elizabeth went out to pray by the great crucifix that stood in the cloister quadrangle. Mother Germaine found her there, standing motionless in the quiet evening air. "I'm passing into the soul of my Christ," Elizabeth said.

Postulants are always introduced into their new life gradually, and Mother Germaine was especially conscious that Elizabeth's health was not at its best after the strain of waiting. She therefore made sure she had plenty of rest and insisted she eat well. Also, when someone enters the religious life, the pain of parting is felt most deeply by those they leave behind; the postulant has all the adventure of discovering the new life she is entering into, but the family has only the emptiness of the departure. Mother Germaine therefore sent word to Guite and Mme. Catez that they could come and see her. She had entered on a Friday, and her family visited her on Saturday, Sunday, and Monday, so they could see for themselves that Elizabeth was settling in well, before they set off for their much-needed holiday in Switzerland.

As for Elizabeth herself, everything about her new life delighted her. From her very first day she fell in love with her cell, the Carmelite cell she had yearned for so long, and described it in a letter to Framboise:

> Our cell, this little nest loved above all others, is exactly like my bedroom in size, with the bed and the window in the same place, with the door where my chest of drawers was and, in the corner where my dressing room was, our desk, on which I'm writing to you." (L 88)

It was sparsely furnished with a bed, a straw-seated chair, and a writing desk. She also had a small portable desk that she placed on her knees to write on. The floor was of bare boards. There was no heat or running water, and the only light was from a small oil lamp. Above the bed was a large wooden cross painted black without the figure of Christ: the Carmelite was to put herself there. On the white walls were three sepia pictures with a small picture on the door that indicated the sister's name. It was stark and bare, but the very plainness and absence of superfluities gave it a simple, austere beauty and a visual peace.

To Elizabeth it was the outward embodiment of the inner cell she had lived in for so long. As she went into it for the first time, she was heard to murmur, "The Trinity is there!" (SD 12).

The Carmelite life to which Elizabeth was now introduced was a harmonious balance of liturgical and private prayer, work, and recreation. The sisters rose at 5 A.M. and began the day with an hour of private prayer followed by the Divine Office and Mass. There was manual work during the day, with breaks for other hours of the Divine Office; vespers was at 2 P.M., with a rest period until 3 P.M. There were two meals a day, at 10:15 A.M. and 6:05 P.M., and two recreation periods after the morning and evening meals. They retired to bed at 10:50 P.M. Although the horarium has changed to some extent since Elizabeth's day, it is a way of life that, in its essentials, has changed little.

There were seven sisters in the novitiate when Elizabeth entered, most of whom were destined for the Paray-le-Monial Carmel. There were three professed sisters, Marie-Madeleine of Jesus, Marie-Geneviève of the Trinity, and Marie of the Holy Spirit; three novices, Hélène of Jesus, Marie-Angèle of the Child Jesus, and Marie-Odile of the Sacred Heart; and a postulant, Angèle of the Sacred Heart. They went to the novitiate after Mass each day for prayers and to give an account of their prayer, and at 4.30 P.M. they received instruction from their novice mistress.

Elizabeth was given the task of sweeping and dusting the choir and arranging fresh flowers for the altar, a task that delighted her as she was so close to her Lord in the Blessed Sacrament. She also helped Sr. Louise Gonzague, the *robier* (tailor), to make and repair the habits. In a letter to her Rolland aunts, Elizabeth said that these habits were about twenty or thirty years old, having been patched again and again, so there was sometimes little of the original material left. She would collect her work from the robier and take it to her cell, where she delighted in the silence and the simplicity of her surroundings as she sewed:

> ...it is filled with God and I spend such wonderful hours there alone with the Bridegroom. For me, the cell is something sacred, it is His intimate sanctuary, just for Him and His little bride. We are so much "together," I am silent, I listen to Him...it is so good to hear everything He has to say. And I love Him while I ply my needle and work on this dear serge that I have so longed to wear. (L 168)

In the peace and the silence she began to blossom once more. In her letters Elizabeth wanted her family and friends to know that she loved them just as deeply as ever, and that she was truly happy. She was well aware that her mother feared she wouldn't be looked after in Carmel's austere routine, and even more concerned that her daughter's eagerness for self-denial and sacrifice would encourage her to extremes. Elizabeth was at pains to reassure her on all points:

> What happiness it is to come and have a little chat with you. Oh! if you knew how much I love you; it seems to me that I will never be able to thank you enough for letting me enter this dear Carmel where I am so happy. It's partly to you as well that I owe my happiness, for you surely know that if you had not said "yes," your little Sabeth would have stayed close by you. Oh! my little mother, how the good God loves you, if you could see with what tenderness He looks on you!...
>
> Since you want me to tell you about myself, I'm going to make you happy. My health is perfect, my appetite has returned to normal, and I'm doing credit to the cooking of Carmel. Alice told me you would like me to drink a little wine; don't you recall that I can't digest it? I sleep like the blessed on our straw mattress; it's been a long time since I've had that happen. The first night, I didn't feel very secure, and I wondered if I weren't going to roll out; by the next morning, I had already gotten used to our bed. I go to sleep before 9 o'clock, and I wake up at

5:30, isn't that *great*? So I'm recovering. Tonight Mother
Subprioress is letting me go to Matins, and I'm delighted.
You can rest assured, I won't do too much; this good little
Mother cares for me like a real baby. (L 85)

Mother Germaine added a little note of her own at the end: "Dear
Madame, I have really wanted to write to you, to speak to you at
greater length about our dear little Sister, but time has been lacking;
besides, you know my heart so well with regard to her and also to
you. Elizabeth is doing *very well* in all ways, is looking well again
and is perfectly happy. We love her more and more."

Three days later, on August 12, Mother Marie of Jesus arrived
unexpectedly during evening recreation. She had come for the veiling
ceremony of a newly professed sister, Madeleine of Jesus, the
following day. Madeleine would be returning to Paray-le-Monial
with her.

Elizabeth commented: "Do you see this little jealousy: I was quite
pleased that it was not Mother Subprioress who performed the ceremony, for I want to be her first, she is so good, I love her so much"

She added, no doubt aware of the horrors those outside would
think happened in Carmel: "As a *terrible trial*, I had to compose some
verses for the veiling and sing them last night at recreation. I was
shaking...which is really ridiculous, for our Sisters are so charitable
that they found my work a great success" (L 87).

In spite of her nervousness, though, Elizabeth, who had written
verse for herself for the past seven years, enjoyed this enduring
Carmelite custom of writing verses for festive occasions. She sent a
copy of these, her first verses in Carmel, to her family; the short four
line stanzas are written to a jaunty little meter that happily reflects her
inner joy.

That day for the first time Mother Subprioress let her get up at five
o'clock: "I was afraid I wouldn't be able to dress in a quarter of an
hour, so you can imagine how pleased I was to find I was the first to
arrive in choir!" Her postulant's dress was far simpler to put on than
the full habit.

She filled her letters with accounts of the small happenings of her new life; there was the time a bat got into her cell during the Great Silence, for example, and she had to knock on Mother Germaine's cell next door to help her remove it; or the time she fell asleep during the night office and was packed off to bed. At the end of August she helped with the wash for the first time:

> For the occasion I put on my nightcap, my brown dress all turned up, a large apron over that and, to complete the outfit, our wooden shoes. I went down like that to the laundry room where they were scrubbing for all they were worth, and I tried to do like the others. I splashed and soaked myself all over, but that didn't matter, I was thrilled! Oh, you see, everything is delightful in Carmel, we find God at the wash just as at prayer. Everywhere there is only Him. We live Him, breathe Him. If you knew how happy I am, my horizon grows larger each day. (L 89)

She was a happy Carmelite, echoed Mother Germaine. In entering Carmel she had truly come home and her whole being expanded. She was unimpressed when her family wrote telling her of the wonderful scenery they were traveling through on their holidays.

She wrote back: "I used to love those mountains so much, they spoke to me of Him. But you see, my darlings, the horizons of Carmel are even more beautiful, it is the Infinite!" (L 87).

She put lots of little details in her letters, but when friends asked her about her life in Carmel, she more simply replied, "It is to love and to pray."

The grilles, which those outside found grim and even repelling, were to her the beloved bars that made her "the prisoner of love," as she called it, echoing Thérèse of Lisieux. It was a paradox that the confines of Carmel could open the infinite spaciousness and richness of God to her. Each Sunday there was exposition of the Blessed Sacrament in the oratory:

> I feel that all the treasures enclosed in the soul of Christ are mine, so I feel so rich; and with what happiness I come

to draw from this source for all those I love.... I can't find words to express my happiness, every day I appreciate it more. Here there is no longer anything but Him, He is All; He suffices, and we live by Him alone. We find Him everywhere.... When I open the door and contemplate the divine Prisoner who has made me a prisoner in this dear Carmel, it seems to me that it is almost the gate to Heaven that is opening! (L 91)

She loved the peace and solitude of her cell, especially during the Great Silence that began after compline each evening. She would sit by her window, which overlooked the quadrangle with the great crucifix in the middle and trees beyond, and pray with and for those she loved. Before she left home, Elizabeth had given her sister a crucifix that Guite kept for the rest of her life; it became a meeting place for the two of them, divided by Carmel's walls, but so very close in their mutual prayer. While reminding her sister of their rendezvous, she gives her advice on meditating:

I would advise you to simplify all your reading, to fill yourself a little less, you will see that this is much better. Take your Crucifix, look, listen. You know our rendezvous is there, and don't be troubled when you are occupied like you are now and can't do all your exercises: you can pray to God while working, it's enough to think of Him. Then all becomes sweet and easy since you're not working alone, since Jesus is there. (L 93)

She gave the same rendezvous to her young friend Framboise, too. The fourteen-year-old, highly strung and somewhat spoiled, was throwing temper tantrums at not having Elizabeth with her anymore. "In the past I overlooked these fits of temper, but now you're no longer a baby and these scenes are ridiculous. I know that you'll allow your Sabeth anything, so I'm telling you what I think!" (L 98).

Elizabeth realized the young girl was very much like herself: fiery, energetic, but also sensitive and impressionable: "You see, nothing has changed, I am always your little mother.... Do you want to continue our rendez-vous at 8 P.M...?" "There, between your Crucifix and my picture, since you love it so much, recollect yourself for a moment and imagine that I am there with the good Jesus and my Framboise" (L 98).

This quiet hour between compline and matins was also a time when she wrote letters. Carmelites were allowed to write to their relatives once a month and to friends once every three months, except when visits in the parlor replaced letters. However, there were always exceptions, especially in the first months of postulancy when letters meant so much to those left behind. In keeping with her spirit of poverty, Elizabeth used a great variety of writing paper, much of it given to the community and mostly of poor quality: a Dijon notary donated some of his notepaper, for example. She would carefully cut unused pieces of paper from correspondence or wherever she found it, used the back of old sermon notes, wrapping paper, old visiting cards, and even the backs of chocolate wrappers. Only elderly or sick people like her Rolland aunts or Mme. Angles were treated with the better quality paper.

Considering the circumstances, she wrote an unusually large volume of letters during her few years in Carmel, but these were almost an extension of her prayer, and her prioress undoubtedly recognized that she was fulfilling a real apostolate through them. In them she revealed her spiritual development that might otherwise have remained mostly unexpressed, and the world might have been much poorer.

Mother Marie of Jesus' term of office as the prioress at Dijon came to an end in October, and she returned to the community for the elections on October 9. To Elizabeth's great joy, Mother Germaine was elected prioress and her "angel," Marie of the Trinity, was elected subprioress.

Mother Germaine, born in Dijon, was thirty-one at this time. She was to remain in office for the whole of Elizabeth's time in Carmel and was the best possible guide for her in her path to holiness. She was an outstanding Carmelite, prayerful, peaceful, and with a rich and loving heart. She was also shy and somewhat diffident about her abilities at the head of her community. She set as her goal at the start of her term as prioress to keep the Carmelite observance as perfectly as possible, but she had the flexibility and wisdom to know when to make exceptions.

Mother Marie of Jesus returned to Paray-le-Monial the day after the elections, taking with her three more sisters from the novitiate. Ten sisters had now gone to Paray, with twenty sisters left in Dijon. Since there were now only three sisters in the novitiate, Hélène of Jesus, Geneviève of the Trinity, and Elizabeth herself, Mother Germaine decided to take over the role of novice mistress.

Elizabeth was delighted. A close and loving bond had already been established between them. Ardent and generous in their self-giving, both shared a deep love of the Carmelite life. Mother Germaine was also a great admirer of Thérèse of Lisieux and made her teachings the inspiration of the novitiate. She was also a true "mother" and provided the loving, self-giving environment Elizabeth needed for her spiritual journey.

A few days later, October 15, the community celebrated the feast of St. Teresa of Avila with exposition of the Blessed Sacrament. Elizabeth spent much time in prayer, her most fervent prayer being that she should soon be allowed to go forward to her clothing and put on the brown Carmelite habit she had yearned to wear for so long. She received inner assurance that she would be clothed on the feast of the Immaculate Conception, December 8, although the period of postulancy was normally six months, and she would have been in Carmel only four months.

She spoke of it the following day to Mother Germaine, who replied that she had to prove herself worthy of it first. This was a very dampening reply, but the prioress was well aware that the community's initial skepticism about Elizabeth's exceptional prayer life had given way to awareness that she really was genuine, and they had a deep affection and love for her.

Even so, when the chapter sisters met a month later to discuss her clothing, and Elizabeth was to present her petition, Mother Germaine said: "I don't know what the good God and the community will decide, but prepare to accept the decision with peace, whatever it is. You have a lot to learn, and perhaps you will be asked to wait a little longer."

"I know I have a long way to go," Elizabeth replied, "but I believe the good God wants to give me this grace. As for my sisters, how could they possibly refuse me? They must love me, as I love them so much" (Souv. 91).

The community voted unanimously to accept her for clothing, and the date was fixed for December 27. However, Abbé Vallée, who was to preach the sermon, was unable to be there on that day, and it was inconvenient for the family also; it was finally fixed for December 8, as Elizabeth had been assured it would be. She wrote to Canon Angles:

> I am so very happy to announce to you my immense happiness, to which, I know, you have contributed a large part. Do I need to express my profound gratitude.... On the 8th, that beautiful feast of her Immaculate Conception, Mary is going to clothe me in my dear Carmelite habit. I will prepare myself for the beautiful day of my betrothal by a three-day retreat. Oh! you see, when I think about it, I already feel as if I am no longer on earth! Pray much for your little Carmelite, that she may be wholly surrendered, wholly given, and that she may give joy to her Master's Heart.... Ask Him that I might live no longer but that He might live in me. (L 99)

A community retreat was given by Abbé Vergne, S.J., in November, and shortly afterward on December 5, Elizabeth started her three-day retreat. On the day itself she spent the morning in the extern quarters with her family and friends. Then, dressed in her white satin bridal dress, she went to the chapel for the first part of the clothing ceremony that was presided over by the Bishop of Dijon, Msgr. Le Nordez. Then she went through to the choir to be clothed in the habit.

Her joy that day was ecstatic. "I cannot bear such joy," she was heard to murmur, and at recreation that evening she celebrated her happiness in the customary verses she had composed for the occasion. The many verses summed up her spiritual life and thoughts thus far; she was a prisoner of love within the Trinity, wrapped in the white cloak of purity, the brown habit symbolizing her unworthiness:

Allow me, this lovely day,
Allow me to sing my Love,
Love that made me prisoner
To consume me through and through.
See me now betrothed,
Clothed in humble garb,
Wrapped in a white mantle
Following the Lamb....
How good it is in the Trinity,
All is light and love.
Christ, who deigned to choose me,
Take me, no more to part. (P 74)

8

CAPTIVE OF THE DIVINE CAPTIVE
Novitiate

> I no longer live, he lives in me,
> I see him face to face;
> Vision nothing can dispel
> Not even the night of faith. (P 75)

This verse came in a poem Elizabeth wrote at Christmas later that month. It was a foreshadowing of a difficult year ahead of her; in contrast to the joy and enthusiastic delight of her postulancy, her novitiate would be a hard test.

The year as a novice is meant to be a time of testing for the community to find out if the young nun is serious in her vocation, and for the novice to find out if this is the life she really wants. Today, after the year of novitiate proper, the religious takes temporary vows for three years and can leave at any time without difficulty during that period leading up to her final vows. But in Elizabeth's time, the first vows were also final, although the sister remained in the novitiate for a further three years before joining the community as a full chapter sister.

The novice was expected to live the full Carmelite day, which was very demanding, although there could be occasional relaxations, of course. Faults and failings were pointed out that might have been overlooked in the postulancy.

For the moment, though, her joy was undimmed, and she wrote to her Rolland aunts that she was as happy as a fish in water. She made light of the often harsh conditions of her first winter in Carmel. The monastery was unheated, except for a fire in the community room, and her delicate skin soon became chilblained. And she mentioned only in passing the blisters on her hands that were caused by her vigorous scrubbing at the community wash. She had to apologize for the poor writing in her letters in the winter, too; there was only the inadequate light of an oil lamp to see by, and her bandaged fingers were clumsy in holding the pen. But she dismissed the severe cold in reply to Mme. Angles:

> You ask me how I can endure the cold. Do believe that I am no more generous than you are, only you are ill, whereas I am in good health. I do not feel the cold. So you see, I have little merit, and I used to suffer much more from winter at home than I do in Carmel where I have no heat at all. God gives the grace; besides, it is so good, when one feels these little things, to look at the Master who also endured all that because He "loved us exceedingly," as Saint Paul says; then one thirsts to repay Him love for love! In Carmel we find many sacrifices of this kind, but they are so sweet when the heart is wholly taken by love. (L 156)

So she simply wrapped her blistered hands in scraps of rag, exclaimed with delight at the beauty of the patterned hoarfrost on the cloister windows, and accepted the discomforts with her usual simplicity and lack of fuss. It was for self-sacrifice and total giving that she had entered Carmel. In February, a family friend, Mme. de Bobet, sent her a copy of the works of St. John of the Cross, and his writings helped her to penetrate more deeply into the spiritual meaning of her self-giving. Quoting from his works she wrote:

> Most beautiful of creatures, who desires so ardently to know the dwelling place of your Beloved in order to seek Him and be united with Him, you are yourself the refuge where He takes shelter, the dwelling place in which He hides Himself. Your Beloved, your Treasure, your one Hope is so close to you as to live within you; and, actually, you cannot have life without him! (St. John of the Cross, *Spiritual Canticle*, 1, 7).
>
> That is the whole life of Carmel, to live in Him. Then all sacrifices, all immolations become divine, for through everything the soul sees Him whom it loves, and everything leads it to Him; it is a continual heart-to-heart! You see you can already be a Carmelite in soul. Love silence and prayer, for that is the essence of Carmelite life. (L 136)

On January 13 one of the sisters, Marie of the Cross, who had been confined to the infirmary for some time, died at the age of sixty-two. A death in Carmel, although sorrowful, is also shot through with a sense of triumph and joy that a sister has "made it" after her years of quiet fidelity and prayer. In Elizabeth the experience of death reawakened her desire to die of love, as she expressed it in a short verse:

> My Beloved, when will my turn come?
> When will you take one who hungers for you?
> She pines, wounded by your love.
> To die, yes, to die of love! (P 76)

This homesickness for heaven was still preoccupying her when she wrote a letter to Mother Marie of Jesus just before Lent:

> Oh! my good Mother, offer a few prayers that the little "house of God" might be wholly filled, wholly invaded by the Three! I have set off into the soul of my Christ, and there I am going to spend my Lent. Ask Him that I might live no longer, but that He might live in me, that the "One" might be consumed more every day, that I might always remain beneath the great vision! It seems to me that this is the secret of sanctity, and it is so simple! Oh my good Mother, to think that we have our Heaven within us, that Heaven for which I am sometimes homesick.... How good it will be when the veil is lifted at last, and we have the joy of being face to face with Him whom alone we love! In the meantime I live in love, I am immersed in it, I am lost in it. It is the Infinite, that infinity for which my soul is starving. (L 107)

Mother Germaine of Jesus let her break the Lenten silence, when no letters were normally allowed, to write to Guite for her birthday on February 20, and she developed this thought further: her life is heaven in anticipation. Her longing was not for something she didn't yet have, but only for its full possession. This idea was fundamental to Elizabeth's spirituality and she pursues it with a direct and simple logic:

> Let us live with God as with a friend, let us make our faith
> a living faith in order to be in communion with Him
> through everything, for that is what makes saints. We pos-
> sess our Heaven within us, since He who satisfies the hun-
> ger of the glorified in the light of vision gives Himself to
> us in faith and mystery, it is the Same One! It seems to me
> that I have found my Heaven on earth, since Heaven is
> God, and God is [in] my soul. The day I understood that,
> everything became clear to me. (L 122)

For Elizabeth, this was not just a lovely spiritual idea; once she understood it, she lived it with unrelenting persistence; as she said herself, it was how saints were made. It was a way that was typical of her, since there was no dividing line between her spiritual life and her everyday life. In her letter to Guite Elizabeth went on to reassure her family, who were worried by the thought of the hard Lenten observance in Carmel: "Lent isn't tiring me; I don't even notice it, and then I have a good little Mother who watches over me with a quite *maternal* heart" (L 109).

There were joys as well as sorrows that year. On June 15 they celebrated their first feast for Mother Germaine on her name day, and Elizabeth wrote beforehand to Guite, asking her to find various pieces of music for her, probably so she could put her verses to the music, and also for some kid-glove leather with which to make gifts. The celebrations were shadowed somewhat, though, when Hélène of Jesus, one of her companions in the novitiate, left a few days later to return to her family. Elizabeth wrote to her affectionately shortly afterward:

> May Christ bring us into those depths, those abysses
> where one lives only by Him. Would you like to be united
> to your little sister in order to become wholly loving,
> wholly listening, wholly adoring?
> To love, to love all the time, to live by love, that is, to
> be surrendered. (L125)

Then the following month, she heard the good news that Guite had become engaged. Her fiancé was Georges Chevignard, a thirty-two-year-old banker. Elizabeth had once confided to Canon Angles that she hoped her sister, too, might have a Carmelite vocation; obviously now that was not to be, but when she saw Guite shortly after the announcement, she saw her sister radiantly happy with a joy that had been quenched for a year or more. She wrote to her mother on the anniversary of her entry into Carmel: "Oh! let me tell you that I am happy, *divinely happy*, that God has been *too good* to me; it's all a wave that overflows in my soul, a wave of gratitude and love toward Him and toward you: thank you for having [given] me to Him" (L 130).

When her future brother-in-law came to visit her a little later on, she pronounced him to be "a pearl among brothers-in-law!" Of a similarly serious disposition as Guite, he was kind, thoughtful, and caring, and it was to be a happy marriage.

In June of that year Mother Germaine gave Elizabeth a "spiritual brother," Abbé Beaubis, a seminarian in the Dijon seminary who was to go out to China as a missionary. Teresa of Avila had founded her Carmels with the specific task of praying for priests, and there has always been a close bond between priests and Carmels. It intensified the fervor of Elizabeth's apostolic prayer. Teresa wrote: "And when your prayers, desires, disciplines, and fasts are not directed toward obtaining these things I mentioned, reflect on how you are not accomplishing or fulfilling the purpose for which the Lord brought you here together" (St. Teresa of Avila, *The Way of Perfection*, 3:10).

"Pray that I might have his passion for God and for souls," added Elizabeth, "for a Carmelite must be an apostle." The Carmelite prays and strives for the closest possible union with God, not simply for her own holiness and salvation; she is aware that the more she is living in Christ, the more powerful she is in her prayer for others. Just as evil can pollute and corrupt, even more so can goodness and holiness transform. Elizabeth herself expressed it in the first letter she wrote to Abbé Beaubis:

> Oh, how powerful over souls is the apostle who remains always at the Spring of living waters; then he can

overflow without his soul ever becoming empty, since he lives in communion with the Infinite! I am praying fervently for you, that God may invade all the powers of your soul, that He may make you live in communion with His whole Mystery, that everything in you may be divine and marked with His seal, so that you may be another Christ working for the glory of the Father! You are praying for me too, aren't you? I want to be an apostle with you, from the depths of my dear solitude in Carmel, I want to work for the glory of God, and for that I must be wholly filled with Him; then I will be all-powerful: one look, one desire [will] become an irresistible prayer that can obtain everything, since it is, so to speak, God whom we are offering to God. May our souls be one in Him and, while you bring Him to souls, I will remain, like Mary Magdalene, silent and adoring, close to the Master, asking Him to make your word fruitful in souls. "Apostle, Carmelite," it is all one! Let us be wholly His, Monsieur l'Abbé, let us be flooded with His divine essence, that He may be the Life of our life, the Soul of our soul, and we may consciously remain night and day under His divine action. (L 124)

Although community life and observance continued in quiet and uninterrupted flow, circumstances were already beginning to threaten its very existence. The Law of Associations that had come into effect the previous July required religious establishments to register with the authorities. Many priests, monks, and nuns were forced to flee, their schools, colleges, and religious houses closed down. In the April and May elections the Waldeck-Rousseau government was elected to power, with Emile Combes elected president of the council. The administration followed an extremely hard-line antireligious policy, forcing thousands of religious to leave the country.

The Dijon community refused to apply for authorization and simply sat tight, expecting to be expelled at any moment. They did start taking steps, though, in case they were forced to leave. Elizabeth wrote to her mother asking for a skirt pattern and materials for them to make into secular clothes, and toward the end of the year Mother Germaine went to Switzerland to look at a house in Charmey that had been offered to them.

All this was very distressing for Elizabeth, with the community life she loved so much at risk, but also to know how worried her family was. It was especially hard because they had thought that at least she was near them in Dijon; now she might be forced to live even further away. Also, Guite and Georges were married, much to Elizabeth's delight, on October 15, the feast of St. Teresa of Avila. This was a joy to her mother, but it also meant that she was now alone, with both her daughters gone.

Mme. Catez had never become reconciled to Elizabeth being in Carmel. Her hopes that Elizabeth might come out once she had tried it for a while were fading as she seemed so completely happy, and Mme. Catez hated the forbidding grilles in the parlor that inhibited any real intimacy.

This conflict between her religious life and her family was probably one factor in an increasing confusion of mind that Elizabeth now began to experience, although she never allowed it to surface in any of the letters she wrote. As she spoke of her difficulties only to her prioress and her confessors, the details of her inner struggle are not clear, but it seems she was experiencing problems in her emotional life that caused her deep distress. She struggled through the summer months and hoped that the community retreat preached by Abbé Vallée in the eight days leading up to the feast of St. Teresa would provide the breakthrough and the refreshment she needed. At one time she would have reveled in the retreat, but now, to her despair, it made her inner darkness even harder to bear. She hoped that Abbé Vallée, who had helped and inspired her so much in the past, would be able to advise her, but he was completely unable to understand what was happening to her. On the contrary, he wondered whether the Carmel was to blame. Finding her so changed from the happy, lively person she had once been, he exclaimed sadly as he came out of the parlor, "What have you done to Elizabeth?"

What was happening to her? There were undoubtedly many factors at work, besides the external uncertainty already described. The scruples that had distressed her in her early teens might have returned. As her letters amply testify, she had the highest of ideals and a profound awareness of the spiritual life, and she was striving with all her heart to realize them in her life. The gulf between our ideals and our ability to put them into practice will be immense for most of us, and Elizabeth was perhaps relying too much, as she had then, on her strong will. When she experienced her inevitable failures, she very likely judged herself too harshly.

She was profoundly conscious of her own weakness and unworthiness, but she had to learn by hard and painful experience just how true that really was. She was highly gifted in prayer and spiritual awareness, but she had to learn how totally they were a gift from God and not her own achievement. Also, because prayer normally came so easily to her, she didn't understand that for most people prayer was a struggle much of the time, easy only on occasion. When she had experienced struggles herself, she had much more understanding of the difficulties in prayer that others faced. There were times, as she confessed to Mother Germaine, when prayer was so repugnant to her that she was tempted to walk out. Instead, she persevered.

In a questionnaire she completed at recreation a few days after she had entered, she listed "sensitivity" as her "dominant fault." This sometimes revealed itself in an oversentimentality toward her friends, for example; and although she longed intensely to suffer for her Master, her sensitivity could be deeply hurt by the public corrections that were very much a part of novitiate training, although she never in any way betrayed her hurt. But it was absolutely certain that God was using these problems to purify and temper her. As she herself was so profoundly aware, God had showered her with gifts, and to whom much is given, much will be required. She wanted to give absolutely everything, and these trials were to deepen and strengthen her in union with God. By proving herself faithful at this time, God was increasing her capacity for the terrible Calvary that was to be hers.

The time for her profession was drawing near; this normally took place a year and a day after the clothing, but perhaps because Mother Germaine was away in Switzerland, it was not until December 22 that Elizabeth left the enclosure to be questioned by the bishop's delegate in the extern quarters. He had to satisfy himself as to the earnestness of her decision and the freedom with which she was making her commitment. Afterward she was able to spend a couple of hours with her family, the last time they would see her without being separated by the grilles.

It wasn't a happy time. Georges took photographs of her, as well as of Guite and Mme. Catez. They show Elizabeth with eyes swollen from a mixture of fatigue from her inner battles and the stress of the occasion. She posed, stiff and unsmiling, with her mother and sister; Guite was clutching a handkerchief.

Mme. Catez also had a professional photographer, Mazillier, to take some pictures as well. The extern sisters put the black veil of the professed sister on her; M. Mazillier thought the simple austerity of the chapel entrance needed livening up a bit, so he had her stand behind an ornate and inappropriate prie-dieu, with a hastily laid rug on the patterned tiles. Elizabeth was obviously ill at ease in the artificial setting; her face and posture were frozen and totally lacking in her usual grace and radiant serenity.

Two days later on Christmas Eve, Mother Germaine told her that the community had unanimously accepted her for profession. Joy can and often does exist with suffering, and Elizabeth's happiness at the news was deep and genuine. She wrote to Mme. Angles:

> It cannot be put into words, but your soul has been in close enough communion with God to understand it.... I feel my weakness, but He is within me to prepare me; so, wholly joyful and confident, I will dare to go before Him so He may consummate the union He has dreamed of in His infinite love. (L 149)

The date was fixed for January 11, which that year was the feast of the Epiphany, a feast "full of light and adoration" for her. As she went into her ten day retreat in preparation for the great day, though, what light she experienced turned to ever-increasing darkness. By the eve of her profession, her anguish was so intense that she left a note on Mother Marie of the Trinity's stool to tell her former "angel" that she had been to see Mother Germaine, who felt uneasy about allowing her to make her vows in such a distressed state of mind. The prioress called in the Jesuit priest, Abbé Vergne, to talk with Elizabeth, and he was able to reassure her sufficiently to enable her to go ahead. She spent the night keeping vigil in prayer. She wrote later to Canon Angles:

> During the night that preceded the great day, while I was in choir awaiting the Bridegroom, I understood that my Heaven was beginning on earth; Heaven in faith, with suffering and immolation for Him whom I love! (L 169)

The following morning she went down to the chapter room where, before the whole community, she made her vows of poverty, chastity, and obedience. She then returned to her cell to spend the day in silent prayer until she joined the sisters at the recreation held in her honor.

> I would like to speak to you about my profession, but, you see, it is something *so divine*, earthly language is powerless to repeat it. I had had very beautiful days before, but now I no longer even dare compare them with that day. It was a unique day, and I believe that if I found myself before God, I would not experience any emotion greater than what I felt; what happens between God and the soul at that time is so great! The ceremony is completely private, it takes place in chapter, and the veiling doesn't take place on the same day; I did not explain that to you very well, there are two ceremonies. I hope to receive the veil on the 21st for the feast of Saint Agnes, but it hasn't been decided yet for we don't know if his Excellency will be free that day. (L 154)

In actual fact, the sisters were trying to ensure that the bishop would definitely not be free that day. Dijon was in turmoil at his lack of prudence in running his diocese; it was rumored—falsely—that he was a Freemason. The Dijon Carmel were in profound disagreement with his republican sympathies. So it was decided that, even though as a family friend it would be expected that he should preside at

Elizabeth as novice, with her mother and sister (Guite), on December 22, 1902, the day of her canonical examination before profession of vows.

Elizabeth holding her profession crucifix. She made her final profession of vows on January 11, 1903, the feast of the Epiphany.

Elizabeth's veiling, under the circumstances it was best if he did not do so. The ceremony duly took place, therefore, on January 21, when he was away. At her profession Elizabeth received the large crucifix, the symbol of a Carmelite's dedication, which is worn under the scapular. On the feast of St. Agnes she received the black veil, a symbol of her lifelong commitment to Christ. She wrote:

> "At last He is all mine, and I am all His: now I have nothing else but Him, He is my All!" And now I have only one desire, to love Him, *to love Him all the time*, to be zealous for His honor as a true bride, to give Him joy, to make Him happy by preparing a dwelling and a refuge for Him in my soul. (L 156)

9

HARMONIOUS SOLITUDE
Profession

With her profession, Elizabeth's peace of mind returned. Sr. Geneviève of the Trinity's brother had, some time before, offered them a secondhand camera with all the necessary equipment; she was now the community photographer, and the photographs she took of Elizabeth after her profession are in marked contrast to those taken at her canonical examination. She is relaxed, the light is back in her eyes, and a smile is on her lips. She is "HAPPY," she wrote to Mme. de Sourdon, putting the words in big capitals (L 157).

Shortly after her profession, although she continued to work in the robe room, she was also made second "turn sister," Mother Marie of the Trinity being the sister in charge. The turn sisters assist with visitors and workers coming to the monastery and interact with the extern sisters while remaining within the enclosure. She was unfailing in her kindness and approachability in helping them. When one of the sisters apologized for calling on her so often, she replied: "Don't say that, I'm only too happy to be of some service to you. I want you to forget that you can't come in and fetch what you need yourself" (Souv. 121).

It meant a lot of activity and contact, not only with people outside, but also with sisters in the community. But for Elizabeth, it was her inner life of union with God that was her real work in Carmel. She wrote to Framboise: "the life of a Carmelite is a communion with God from morning to evening, and from evening to morning. If He did not fill our cells and our cloisters, ah! how empty they would be! But through everything, [we] see Him, for we bear Him within us, and our life is an anticipated Heaven" (L 123).

This intense awareness of God made her love silence. The sisters in the novitiate often made "silence challenges" that Elizabeth invariably won. The only time she broke her silence was when someone needed her help. This silence wasn't simply an external thing but went into the depths of her being in a profound absorption in God. One of her fellow novices saw her sweeping one day and wished to speak to her. As she approached her, though, she was so awed by Elizabeth's complete absorption in prayer that she went away, her message undelivered.

Some of the older sisters were still unconvinced that her depth of prayer was genuine, though, and continued to reserve judgment. One of them, possibly Aimée of Jesus, who had a cell next to Elizabeth, said:

> When I heard it said that no one had discovered a single imperfection in Sister Elizabeth of the Trinity, I wanted to prove it for myself, for I wasn't predisposed toward her. A certain worldly polish, the ability to express herself easily, added to her intelligence and a loving nature could, I felt, give her the appearance of a high degree of perfection as yet untested. Although we saw quite a bit of each other, when others spoke of her virtue I had my reservations, not willing to acknowledge it was so complete or so unfailing. So much so that one day Mother Subprioress said to me "You don't like Sr. Elizabeth, do you?" "I like her very much," I replied, "but I'm waiting before I say anything." "Well," she replied, "I can only say that when she has been corrected I have always found her very gentle and humble."
>
> After that I studied her even more closely and was at last obliged to admit that I never found the least fault in her. Some might think this is an exaggeration, but it is the truth.
>
> She was never rigid or narrow but always humble and unassuming and with her share of unintentional faults and weaknesses; I never saw her give in to herself. She always seemed to me to be not only faith-ful but I would even say heroic in some extremely difficult circumstances.
>
> My cell was next to hers, and I used to hear her get up every morning as soon as the signal had sounded. When she reached the choir or oratory she would kneel down and seem to be lost in God. She would remain motionless however tired her knees might be or, later, however ill she was. (Souv. 127–128)

Elizabeth in the white Carmelite choir mantle, holding her breviary. This photograph as well as the following one and the one on the cover were taken in the monastery garden in January–February 1903. (Snow is visible on the ground.)

Elizabeth in monastery garden in early 1903. She is holding her *Manual*, open at the New Testament.

This sister also suffered from severe headaches and Elizabeth, knowing this, moved so quietly about her cell that she never once disturbed her. It was in these small and almost mundane ways that Elizabeth expressed her union with God. She was increasing in assurance, too, when writing to her friends and acquaintances and sharing her understanding of the spiritual life with them. She didn't think that her life as an enclosed nun was so different from the life of her friends in the world that she had nothing to offer them. Before entering she had said that she would live the life of a Carmelite in the world; now she urged them to discover for themselves the insights she was discovering from living in Carmel. Despite their very different lifestyles, Elizabeth in Carmel and her friends outside were endeavoring to live the fullness of the Christian life. And the basis of that was very simple and very fundamental: it was love, love of God expressed in self-giving love for others, lived out in faithfulness to what God wanted of each one as individuals. Elizabeth could easily apply what she was discovering in Carmel to the needs of the people she was writing to.

In writing to Framboise about prayer, for example, she could speak very simply and practically. Her own degree of prayer was high, but in its essentials it was no different from what she recommended to the temperamental young girl:

> Yes, my darling, I am praying for you and I keep you in my soul quite close to God, in that little inner sanctuary where I find Him at every hour of the day and night. I'm never alone: my Christ is always there praying in me, and I pray with Him. You grieve me, my Framboise; I can well see that you're unhappy and I assure you it's your own fault. Be at peace. I don't believe you're crazy, just nervous and overexcited, and when you're like that, you make others suffer too. Ah, if I could teach you the secret of happiness as God has taught it to me. You say I don't have any worries or sufferings; it's true that I'm very happy, but if you only knew that a person can be just as happy even when she is crossed. We must always keep our eyes on God. In the beginning it's necessary to make an effort when we're just boiling inside, but quite gently, with patience and God's help, we get there in the end.

You must build a little cell within your soul as I do. Remember that God is there and enter it from time to time; when you feel nervous or you're unhappy, quickly seek refuge there and tell the Master all about it. Ah, if you got to know Him a little, prayer wouldn't bore you any more; to me it seems to be rest, relaxation. We come quite simply to the One we love, stay close to Him like a little child in the arms of its mother, and we let our heart go. You used to love sitting very close to me and telling me your secrets; that is just how you must go [to] Him; if only you knew how well He understands.... You wouldn't suffer any more if you understood that. (L 123)

To Germaine de Gemeaux, who was herself considering the religious life, she could write with greater depth about her understanding of the Carmelite life:

A Carmelite, my darling, is a soul who has *gazed on the Crucified*, who has seen Him offering Himself to His Father as a Victim for souls and, recollecting herself in this great vision of the charity of Christ, has understood the passionate love of His soul, and has wanted to give herself as He did!... And on the mountain of Carmel, in silence, in solitude, in prayer that never ends, for it continues through everything, the Carmelite already lives as if in Heaven: "by *God alone*." The same One who will one day be her beatitude and will fully satisfy her in glory is already giving Himself to her. He never leaves her, He dwells within her soul; more than that, the two of them are *but one*. So she *hungers for silence* that she may always listen, penetrate ever deeper into His Infinite Being. She is identified with Him whom she loves, she finds Him everywhere; she sees Him shining through all things! Is this not Heaven on earth! You carry this Heaven within your soul, my little Germaine, you can be a Carmelite already, for Jesus recognizes the Carmelite from *within*, by her soul. Don't ever leave Him, do everything beneath His divine gaze, and remain wholly joyful in His peace and love, making those around you happy! (L 133)

It was in writing to priests, though, that she revealed the depth of her spiritual life. She felt a very real bond with them, because she was strongly aware of the priestly nature of her own calling as a Christian who, by her baptism, shares in the priesthood of Christ himself. Some of her most profound letters were written to André Chevignard, Georges's brother. He was studying for the priesthood at the Dijon seminary and was ordained to minor orders on March 28, 1903. Elizabeth wrote to him for the first time just before Lent began:

> Before entering into the great silence of Lent, I want to answer your kind letter. And my soul needs to tell you that it is wholly in communion with yours, letting itself be caught, carried away, invaded by Him whose charity envelops us and who wishes to consummate us into "one" with Him. I thought of you when I read these words of Père Vallée on contemplation: "The contemplative is a being who lives in the radiance of the Face of Christ, who enters into the mystery of God, not in the light that flows from human thought, but in that created by the word of the Incarnate Word." Don't you have this passion to listen to Him? Sometimes it is so strong, this need to be silent, that one would like to know how to do nothing but remain like Magdalene, that beautiful model for the contemplative soul, at the feet of the Master, eager to hear everything, to penetrate ever deeper into this mystery of Charity that He came to reveal to us. Don't you find that in action, when we are in Martha's role, the soul can still remain wholly adoring, buried like Magdalene in her contemplation, staying by this source like someone who is starving; and this is how I understand the Carmelite's apostolate as well as the priest's. Then both can radiate God, give Him to souls, if they constantly stay close to this divine source. It seems to me that we should draw so close to the Master, in such communion with His soul, to identify ourselves with all its movements, and then go out as He did, according to the will of His Father. (L 158)

The "passion to listen to him." Sometimes Elizabeth was afraid her prayer was too passive, especially when, before a big feast, for example, the other sisters would discuss what things they would do in the way of novenas, rosaries, or acts of sacrifice. "Oh, for you it's silence, isn't it?" they would remark teasingly when it was her turn, and she would nod with a slight smile (Souv. 133).

It did worry her, though, and after she had listened to the other novices making plans for a Forty Hours devotion, when the Blessed Sacrament would be exposed for prayer, she went to choir resolved to be more active in her prayer. But as soon as she knelt down, her usual profound silence in the presence of God enveloped her, and she received inner confirmation that this was indeed her special gift, the form of prayer most suited to her, and it no longer troubled her.

Elizabeth ended her letter to Abbé Chevignard with a quotation from St. Paul, that she wished "to be hidden with Christ in God." This was a small indication of the growing interest she had in Paul's writings, as well as an increased understanding of Scripture as a whole.

It was the custom in Carmel that before starting in the mornings, the sisters spent about a quarter of an hour reading a short passage from the *Imitation of Christ* and from the Scriptures, especially the Gospels. Up till now Elizabeth had done this dutifully but without any real enthusiasm. The Scriptures didn't play a very big part in her spiritual reading; many passages meant a great deal to her, though, and her spirituality was profoundly scriptural because the priests whose sermons she had followed and the writings of her favorite spiritual masters were permeated by Scripture. Now, though, they were beginning to be her main source of spiritual food, especially her "beloved Paul," as she called him.

Because of its contacts with André Chevignard, the Dijon community was very much aware of the continuing troubles in the diocese and in the seminary. Although André's ordination to minor orders went through peacefully enough, there was a great deal of unrest among the seminarians ready to be ordained to the priesthood. They refused to be ordained by Msgr. Le Nordez because of his cooperation with the authorities. When he sent some of them away, the rest went on strike, and only the threat of being forced to enlist in the army persuaded them to return a few days later. Even parents were refusing to allow him to confirm their children.

Other events, too, that should have been occasions for celebration were soured by the continuing political persecution of Catholics. On April 16 the sisters celebrated the golden jubilee of a sister of the white veil, Marie of the Incarnation, who at seventy-three was the oldest sister in the community. She had been paralyzed for five years at that time and was to die only five days after Elizabeth herself. The previous month the Chamber refused authorization to numerous religious orders, ordering their houses to be closed and their goods confiscated. The Dijon community still steadfastly refused to seek authorization, and on the very day of Marie of the Incarnation's jubilee, the Vicar General, M. Marigny, came in the name of Msgr. Le Nordez to close their chapel to the public; it was to remain closed for nearly three years.

At the same time, across town the Christian Brothers were singing a final Benediction before leaving the country to regroup in exile. The Dijon Carmel fully expected their turn to come at any moment. The following month, therefore, Mother Germaine traveled to Belgium where a schoolhouse was being prepared for them at Noiseux in case they, too, had to leave France. For the time being, though, the prioress went primarily to see if some of their movable goods could be stored there.

Under Mother Germaine's strong and faith-filled leadership, the community kept to the quiet routine of their Rule, whatever the uncertainties of the future. Undoubtedly the spirit in which Elizabeth met the challenge was that of the whole community, a spirit she expressed in a letter to her Rolland aunts:

> Faith is so good; it is Heaven in darkness, but one day the veil will be lifted and we will contemplate in His light Him whom we love; while awaiting the Bridegroom's "Veni" [Come] we must spend ourselves, suffer for Him, and, above all, love Him greatly. Thank Him for having called your little Elizabeth to Carmel for the persecution; I do not know what awaits us, and this perspective of having to suffer because I am His delights my soul. I love my dear cloister so much, and sometimes I have wondered if I don't love this dear little cell too much, where it is so good to be "alone with the Alone." Perhaps one day He will ask me to sacrifice it. I am ready to follow Him everywhere, and my soul will say with Saint Paul: "Who will separate me from the love of Christ?" I

have within me a solitude where He dwells, and nothing can take that away from me! (L 162)

But for the moment they could stay where they were, although they were unable to have their annual retreat that year. The family went off on their holidays as usual; Guite was feeling very tired and unwell, so the Chevignards stayed in the countryside nearby, perhaps at Sainte-Marie-sur-Ouche, while Mme. Catez went to stay with Canon Angles.

When they returned at the beginning of September, her sister happy and rested, her peaches and cream complexion fully restored, the reason for her tiredness was revealed, as well as her overflowing happiness now: she was expecting their first child.

The year drew to a close; shortly after Christmas Elizabeth sat in the peaceful silence of her cell before matins and painted the scene for her Rolland aunts' benefit:

> The sky is beautiful, all clear and starry; the moonlight is flooding our cell through the frosted window panes, it's ravishing; our window looks out over the quadrangle, an interior garden surrounded by our large cloisters; in the middle on a rock a large cross stands out. All is calm and silent, and that makes me think of the night when the little Jesus was given to us. It seems I can hear the Angels singing their sweet canticle: "Rejoice, a Savior has been given to us." Dear Aunts, did you have a nice Christmas? Mine was delightful, for you see, Christmas in Carmel is unique. (L 187)

That outer peace was echoed in a deep inner peace. She wrote to Canon Angles a few days later, and Mother Germaine added a postscript of her own begging his prayers for her "little band" who had a fierce storm raging all around them from the persecutions. But Elizabeth did not allow that storm to penetrate her peace. She spent the time before midnight Mass and Office in choir, she told Canon Angles:

> I loved to say to myself: "He is my All, my one and only All." What happiness, what peace that gives to the soul.

He is the only one, I have given Him all. If I look at it from an earthly point of view, I see solitude and even emptiness, for I cannot say my heart has not suffered; but if my gaze remains always fixed on Him, my luminous Star, oh, then all the rest disappears, and I lose myself in Him like a drop of water in the Ocean. It is all calm, all peaceful, and the peace of God is so good; that is what Saint Paul is speaking of when he says it "surpasses all understanding"! (L 190)

10

PRAYER TO THE TRINITY

Elizabeth did not allow the external storms raging round their Carmel to disturb her inner peace, but this was no selfish isolation. In the turmoil of the political situation her task was to pray, to allow her peace, her union with God, to spread out into the world and bring its hidden healing to the situation. Just as the force of violence and destruction causes its evil to spread, so the power of goodness and love is no less effective, though undoubtedly much less publicized:

> My soul loves to unite with yours in one single prayer for the Church, for the diocese. Since Our Lord dwells in our souls, His prayer belongs to us, and I wish to live in communion with it unceasingly, keeping myself like a little vase at the Source, at the Fountain of life, so that later I can communicate it to souls by letting its floods of infinite charity overflow. "I sanctify myself for them that they also may be sanctified in the truth." Let us make these words of our adored Master all our own, yes, let us sanctify ourselves for souls, and since we are all members of one body, inasmuch as we have an abundance of divine life, we can communicate it in the great body of the Church. (L 191)

In this letter written to Abbé Chevignard, she quotes copiously from St. Paul and concludes, "Let us be united in allowing the power of his love to make us forget all else and become, as St. Paul said, 'the praise of his glory.'" This little phrase, mentioned almost in passing, was to become of immense importance to her in her spiritual development.

Early in Lent, Elizabeth received the good news of the birth of Guite and Georges's first baby. She was born March 11, and the following day Mother Germaine passed around at evening recreation a photograph of her taken by Georges, who was a keen amateur photographer.

"You can imagine how hard my heart was beating," Elizabeth wrote back. "Her soul appears to me like a crystal that radiates the good God, and when I see her I shall kneel and adore him who lives within her." She had to wait until after Easter to see her little niece, though. Before that, she immersed herself in the majestic silence of Holy Week:

> How good it was to keep watch with the Master in the great silence and calm of that night during which He loved us so much.... I could catch a glimpse of the little door of the Tabernacle through my dear grille, and I said to myself: It is really true, I am the prisoner of the divine Prisoner, we are each other's captives! My horizon is expanding...my sky is all calm, all starry, and, in this "harmonious solitude," as my blessed Father Saint John of the Cross says in his *Canticle*, I think God is very good to have taken me all for Himself and set me apart on the mountain of Carmel. That is the hymn of thanksgiving being sung in my soul while I wait to go sing in Heaven, following the Lamb! (L 198)

As soon as Easter arrived, Mme. Catez, "the happy grandmother," came round to give her news of the baby, who had been named after Elizabeth. She was lovingly aware that her mother's loneliness, now that she was by herself in the house, was often like ice around her heart. This new little Elizabeth would be the hundredfold reward her mother now had for giving her daughter to God. Sadly, though, the grandfather, M. Chevignard, was only to enjoy his granddaughter for a short while; he died the following month.

The Chevignards were to have nine children; four of their daughters entered the religious life and one son became a priest. Elizabeth was to follow her aunt into Dijon Carmel, living until she was well into her eighties.

On May 28, M. Beaubis, Elizabeth's "spiritual brother," was ordained and celebrated his first Mass the following day. On June 15, the feast of St. Germaine, the community celebrated the prioress' feast day, a time of relaxation when the sisters make small gifts to give to the prioress that she can then give to friends of the community. The feast of Our Lady of Mount Carmel, July 16, was followed by St.

Martha's day, July 29. On this day the sisters of the white veil, who did not say the Divine Office and who did the domestic work about the monastery, were given the day off, while the novices took over the kitchen.

It seemed as if Elizabeth was the only one in the novitiate at this time, so "my Sister Agnes," Agnes of Jesus and Mary, a professed sister four years older than Elizabeth, helped her. The two of them had become great friends during Lent the previous year when Agnes, who was very artistic and had beautiful handwriting—classic, round, and regular—had helped Elizabeth improve her dreadful handwriting. They laughingly described themselves as David and Jonathan. For St. Martha's day, Elizabeth became the cook and Agnes the provisor, or organizer of the meals.

Guite, who perhaps knew of her sister's limitations as a cook, came to the rescue and supplied them with fresh eggs and an enormous Russian salad prepared by her cook, Fanny, that would last them the following day, too. Elizabeth said she did some amazing things with a cooking pot and vegetables that caused the sisters some hilarity, but hopefully not indigestion.

She wrote to her Rolland aunts, sharing with them once again the snippets of community life which they liked: "I spent a good day at the kitchen stove. Even though I didn't go into ecstasy while holding on to the saucepan handle like St. Teresa, yet I believed the Master's presence was there among us, and deep within myself I adored him whom Magdalene had met in the veil of his humanity" (L 198).

On September 26, she made a ten-day personal retreat, the first since her profession: "I am leaving for my great journey: ten days of complete silence, absolute solitude, with my veil lowered and several additional hours of prayer; it's a very enticing schedule" (L 211). It was also a time of tremendous grace for her; what those graces were will remain her secret, but when she went to Mother Germaine during these days she could only say simply, her voice vainly trying to express the inexpressible and her eyes glowing, "He is giving me eternal life" (Souv. 132).

On October 10, a few days after she came out of retreat, Mother Germaine's term of office came to an end. Elizabeth would not be a full chapter sister and eligible to vote until she had been professed three years and moved from the novitiate into the community, and so she waited with the sisters of the white veil in the antechoir while the elections took place in the choir. To her immense joy, Mother Germaine was reelected for another term of office, with Mother Marie of the Trinity once more her subprioress.

Fears that the community might be forced into exile were receding enough to enable the community to have a preached retreat the following month, given by Abbé Fages, a Dominican priest. Because it was so near Advent, he took that as his theme; it made a powerful impression on Elizabeth, touching as it did on so many aspects that meant a great deal to her. Abbé Fages returned time and again to the Annunciation, when the Holy Spirit overshadowed Mary, waiting in prayer before her God; he linked it to Christians waiting in prayer, eager to bring the Lord to birth within them by grace:

> If you are awaiting the movement of life, formulate your request: "Spirit of God, come upon me as you came down upon the chaos of the world, as you came upon the Virgin Mary to create in her our Lord." Do you want the Word to live in you; do you want the Incarnation to bear its fruit in you? There is only one way. The Holy Spirit caused the Son of God to be conceived and grow in the womb of the Virgin. Well, it is He again who will cause Him to live and grow in you. (Works, v. 1, p. 190, note 26)

During this time the Holy Spirit was working powerfully within Elizabeth, within her prayer. Mother Germaine noticed that it was becoming even more simple, more focused, and profound. "Keep looking at him all the time; keep silent, it is so simple." This silence was far more than absence of noise; it was a deep inner silence when the voice of self is silent and the word of God alone is speaking.

According to Sr. Agnes, some of the sisters sometimes found her single-minded spirituality a little tedious; the same ideas recurred in her poems and conversation. "But she couldn't help it," Agnes remarked, "It was her" (JTD, v. II, p. 268).

Although her spirituality was centered on a fairly narrow range of all the manifold facets of the Christian life, it was nevertheless immensely rich because Elizabeth went unerringly to the great, central mysteries of the faith. She focused on the very being of God himself, bathed in the immensity of the life of the Trinity, of the overflowing love and unbounded richness of her "Three." She was given over to adoration of the God who has revealed himself to us through Jesus Christ, and whose life is communicated to us in the outpouring of the Holy Spirit. No one can ever truly understand fully the profound mystery that he whom the heavens cannot contain actually comes to dwell in us, to share his life with us. Even eternity is not enough for us to exhaust the height, the length, the breadth, and the depth of the life that God has opened out to us in Christ Jesus; as Elizabeth herself loved to say, her horizons were infinite, because they were the horizons of the Most Holy Trinity.

The day after the community retreat ended, she herself expressed this in her most beautiful prayer. It was November 21, 1904, feast of the Presentation of Mary in the temple, the day on which the community renewed their vows. During the course of the day, Elizabeth went to her cell and tore out a page from her personal notebook. Folding the page in half to make it small enough to fit into her "grace book," the small book of community prayers all Carmelites carry with them, she wrote out her prayer without a single correction:

> O my God, Trinity whom I adore, help me to be utterly forgetful of self so as to be rooted in you, as changeless and calm as if I were already in eternity. May nothing disturb my peace or draw me out of you, my unchangeable One, but at every moment may I penetrate ever more deeply into the depths of your mysteries: Make me peaceful, make me your heaven, a home that you love and the place where you can be at rest; may I never leave you there alone, but be there entirely absorbed, in living faith, wholly adoring, freely given up to your creative action.
>
> O my Christ whom I love, crucified by love, I long to be the bride of your heart; I long to cover you with glory and love you...until I die of love. But I realize how weak I am and I beg you to clothe me with yourself, to identify my soul with the movements of your soul. Immerse yourself in me, possess me, substitute yourself for me, that my life becomes but a reflection of your life. Enter into me as Adorer, Restorer and Savior.

Eternal Word, Utterance of my God, I want to spend
my life listening to you. I want to make myself completely open to learn everything from you. Through all the
nights, through every privation and weakness I want to be
with you always, living beneath your blazing light, beloved Star; so fascinate me that I can no longer stray from
your radiance.

Consuming Fire, Spirit of Love, come down upon
me and make me as it were an incarnation of the Word;
may I be another humanity in which he lives out
once more his mystery. And you, Father, bend down
to your poor little creature, cover her with your shadow
and see in her only the Well-Beloved in whom you were
well pleased.

O my "Three," my All, my Bliss, infinite Solitude, Immensity in which I lose myself, I give myself up to you as
your prey; immerse yourself in me that I may be immersed
in you until I go to gaze forever, in your light, on the
boundless depths of your greatness. (NI 15)

This is a prayer for the gift of prayer, and one that God had in great
measure already answered in her. It reveals the form of prayer that
she had been living in ever greater depth since she was a child. So
many of the phrases were simply echoes of what she had pondered
and prayed and written many times over since then. Basically, it is a
self-portrait, but one that God intended to make an even closer likeness in the months ahead.

In community Elizabeth was as self-effacing and unassuming as
ever, affectionately ready to put herself out for her sisters if any needed
help. Mother Germaine made her "angel" to two postulants during
that year—Sr. Madeleine and, on December 15, Sr. Teresa of Jesus.
Her affectionate nature was a great support to the young postulants:
"She knew just how to come to help me," said one of them, "smooth-
ing over my mistakes, gently and humbly making excuses for me,
simply and delicately. She saw to everything and looked after me
constantly like a real 'Tobias'" (Souv. 122).

At the same time she pointed them to the same high ideals she was
living out herself in the most humdrum of daily tasks. "When she
showed me how to look after the novitiate she said, 'Don't treat the

sweeping lightly for it is a little sanctuary here and this is where you'll be starting your Carmelite life.' The way she showed me how to go about my work with a reverence inspired by faith made me realize how much she herself lived in the presence of God and saw in him the smallest things," the postulant added (Souv. 122).

She was always there with a comforting shoulder to cry on when, as sometimes happened, they ended up in tears. But at the same time she would focus their eyes on the crucified Lord they were following, inspiring them with her own longing to suffer with and for him. She herself was the best inspiration for growing in love and union with him.

Her deepening prayer, her constant living in the presence of God, could not but be apparent to others. She wanted to be as transparent as possible to God's life, to allow as little as possible of herself to impede him shining out in all she did and was. A family friend, Mme. Berthe de Goute de Bize, who visited her for the first time in Carmel on February 22, 1905, was moved to tears by her radiant holiness. "I found again her heart perfect," she said later. "The love of God enveloped her completely, but she was able to tell me such tender things.... She had such feelings of affection for her mother that I cried" (L 315, n. 1).

Her increasing absorption in God never made her remote or less loving; indeed, the closer she came to God, the deeper her love and sensitivity grew. The oversensitiveness that she had called her dominant fault, though, was a thing of the past. Early on in her religious life, Mother Germaine had found her spending the time of great silence walking on the terrace, enjoying the quiet evening air. "We do not come to Carmel to dream in the starlight," she told Elizabeth. "Go to God by faith" (SD 16). It was a test of Elizabeth's oversensitivity, but she accepted the rebuke. She never lost her responsiveness and delighted appreciation of the beauties of nature that drew her so instinctively to praise their Creator; indeed, it was second nature to her to see all things in God, whether it was her little niece, the generosity of a friend, or the loveliness of nature. But at the same time her faith continually took her beyond externals.

God is at once revealed to us in created things and yet transcends all that we can understand and think and experience of him. In her prayer Elizabeth sought him whether she could experience his presence or not. Her prayer was not one of continual consolation. Often it was so dry and dark that she was tempted to get up and leave, though no one, seeing her remain motionless for long periods before the Blessed Sacrament on Sundays and feast days, would have guessed it. For her, the light of faith and the obscurity of faith were the same; she went perseveringly beyond them and found God in both.

She could truly say with St. Paul that while her spiritual being was being renewed day after day, her physical being was being worn away. There are small indications of this in her letters. Mother Germaine sometimes added a little note at the end of Elizabeth's letters to her mother, assuring Mme. Catez that her daughter was doing "wonderfully well," especially during Lent; Elizabeth reassured her mother that her health was not suffering from the hot weather in their heavy Carmelite habits. That Christmas, Guite was given permission to give her a warm skirt to wear under her habit to help her through the cold winter. For some time she had been given small dispensations: extra rest sometimes and permission to sit in her choir stall during prayer instead of kneeling or sitting on the floor, as was customary. Her previous energy was gradually giving way to fatigue and stomach problems. In fact, as early as 1903, she had been diagnosed as suffering from Addison's disease.

This disease had only been identified in 1849. It is a condition in which the cortex of the adrenal glands progressively ceases to produce steroid hormones, although the body can compensate for all of them except hydrocortisone. This leads to low levels of glucose, with other symptoms developing gradually, such as loss of appetite and weight, a feeling of increasing tiredness and weakness, anemia, and stomach disorders. At that time it was incurable; although there could be periods of remission, the body eventually destroys the cortex itself, leading to a complete breakdown of the body's immune system. Today it can be kept under control with hydrocortisone tablets.

Until it became acute, the sufferer could lead an almost normal life. It was not widely known during his lifetime, for example, that

President Kennedy suffered from it. Jane Austen died from it, though from her niece Caroline's account it did not seem she suffered acutely. Of her final visit to her aunt she wrote, "I was struck by the alteration in her—She was very pale—her voice was weak and low and there was about her a general appearance of debility and suffering; but I have been told that she never had much actual pain" (Caroline Austen, *My Aunt Jane Austen,* Jane Austen Society, 1952, p. 14). Jane herself spoke of it with the same lightness of touch she used in her novels:

> I certainly have not been well for many weeks, and about a week ago I was very poorly. I have had a good deal of fever at times, and indifferent nights; but am considerably better now and am recovering my looks a little, which have been bad enough—black and white and every wrong color. I must not depend upon being ever very blooming again. Sickness is a dangerous indulgence at my time of life. (*Brabourne Letters of Jane Austen,* v. II, p. 300)

Elizabeth, too, tried to minimize it as much as possible. She never mentioned it in her letters; instead, she was writing to the indispensable Guite about the problem they were having over providing the King's cake for the feast of the Epiphany. This was a special cake that their usual benefactor was unable to supply that year, and the community did not know the recipe for it. As it was a long-standing tradition that they wanted to continue, they accepted Guite's offer to supply it for them.

There were also arrangements to be made for André Chevignard's forthcoming ordination to the diaconate. The community had some beautiful chalice covers that they thought Mme. Catez and Guite might like for him.

André Chevignard would not be ordained by Msgr. Le Nordez. On July 20, 1903, Pope Leo XIII died and was succeeded by Pope Pius X. Because of the continuing unrest in the diocese, the pope finally summoned Le Nordez to Rome. This was one cause, among others, of the French Republic breaking off diplomatic relations with the Holy See in July of that year. On September 4, 1904, Msgr. Le Nordez handed in his resignation as bishop of Dijon. The see was to remain vacant for more than seventeen months.

11

Something Sacred About
Suffering

"May this be a year of love all for the glory of God" (L 218), Elizabeth wrote to Mme. Hallo at the beginning of 1905. Love was also the theme of her New Year's letter to Canon Angles:

> Every day He makes me experience more fully how sweet it is to be His, His alone, and my vocation as a Carmelite moves me to adoration, to thanksgiving. Yes, it is true what Saint Paul says, "He has loved exceedingly," loved His little Elizabeth exceedingly. But love calls forth love, and I ask nothing of God but to understand that knowledge of charity that Saint Paul speaks of and of which my heart wishes to sound the very depths. That will be Heaven, won't it? But it seems to me that we can begin our Heaven even here on earth, since we possess Him, and through everything, we can remain in His love. (L 219)

That meant even in suffering. Just before Lent, she wrote a letter to Canon Angles's sister-in-law, who was having to undergo an operation. Mme. Angles was in her forties at this time and some years before had become traumatized when she had been given insufficient anaesthetic during an operation. Her husband, unable to cope with her condition, had more or less left her, and it was Canon Angles who gave her a home and gently helped her through her mental and physical breakdown to a renewed trust in God. Much later, at the age of seventy-five, she was to enter the Visitation order. Now, understandably, she was dreading the prospect of a further operation. Elizabeth wrote that she fully understood Mme. Angles's apprehensions and prayed that God would calm her fears and give her deep peace. The previous year, when Mme. Angles's health had begun to worsen, Elizabeth had written:

I see the Master is treating you like a "bride" and sharing His Cross with you. There is something so great, so divine in suffering! It seems to me that if the blessed in Heaven could envy anything, it would be that treasure; it is so powerful a lever on the heart of God! And then, don't you find it sweet to give to Him whom you love? The Cross is the heritage of Carmel: "Either to suffer or to die," cried our holy Mother Teresa, and when Our Lord appeared to our Father Saint John of the Cross and asked him what he wanted in return for all the suffering he had endured for Him, John responded: "Lord, to suffer, to be despised for your love." Dear Madame, would you ask that this passion for sacrifice be given to your little friend? For my part, I assure you, I am asking God to sustain you in your sufferings, which must be so painful to endure, for, in the long run, the soul feels the effects of it and grows weary; but then you have only to stay close to the Crucified, and your suffering is the best prayer. (L 207)

There is a telling little phrase here, when Elizabeth says that "in the long run, the soul feels the effects of it and grows weary." Inexorably, her own illness was sapping her strength. She longed desperately to keep the full Lenten observance; "It was very difficult for me to be looked after," she later confided to Mother Germaine, "because I longed so much to follow my Master in self-sacrifice." At the beginning of Lent she asked her prioress if she could have the ordinary collation the community was having.

"You'll take what you are given," replied Mother Germaine, leaving Elizabeth without much hope. She was disappointed at what she thought was a refusal, though of course accepting the prioress's decision. Resisting the temptation to look at her place, while grace was being said at the evening collation, as she slipped into her place she was delighted to see the meager collation she hoped for. "I can't tell you how happy I felt," she went on. "No gourmet could have been more pleased with a sumptuous banquet than I was that evening with my frugal meal" (Souv. 164).

Her spirit might be more than willing, but her body was unable to keep up. It soon became obvious that she was unable to keep the Lenten fast. Her valiant efforts to keep the Rule as fully as possible disguised from the community, though, how seriously ill she really was. In her desire for self-sacrifice, it did not occur to her to ask for more relaxations from her prioress, and it was only later that she spoke to Mother Germaine of the extent of her illness at this time. She felt such utter fatigue as the months passed that without God's help she would have given in. In her duties at the turn, she found it difficult to walk quickly when answering a call. One day she was at the bottom of the stairs when the bell rang, and she had to make a real effort even to climb the first flight; her body simply would not respond. "I can do all things through him who gives me strength," she prayed, in the words of St. Paul, and remembering the example of Carmelites before her somehow managed to force her body to obey her will.

"After reciting the Little Hours in the morning," Elizabeth told her prioress later, "I already felt at the end of my tether and often wondered how I would last out until evening. After compline my cowardice was at its greatest, and I was often tempted to envy a sister who had permission not to go to matins."

"Don't you think you should have had the simplicity to say something to me about how you were feeling?" asked Mother Germaine.

> I just didn't think of it, Mother," Elizabeth replied. "In any case, the exceptions you were already making for me didn't make any difference, so I saw it as God's will for me. Besides, I didn't want to give in to myself and complain and anyway, what more could you have done for me? When you made me rest it didn't help; my whole being was broken down and I couldn't find a comfortable position or enjoy a good night's rest, so that it was a question of whether it was more exhausting for me in the day or the night." (Souv. 174–175)

She would spend the hour of silence before matins in agony, praying in choir, pressed up close to the grille. It gave her enough courage and strength to get through matins, when she was able to keep her mind on God. Then her weakness returned, and she had to struggle back in the darkness to her cell, often holding on to the wall for support.

A long letter she wrote to Mme. Angles toward the end of the year gives a good idea of the spirit with which she faced her illness, and the depth, wisdom, and authority her suffering gave her:

> If you knew how attached my soul is to yours, I would even say how "ambitious" I am for it! I would like it to be wholly surrendered, wholly adhering to that God who loves it with so great a love! ...I believe that the secret of peace and happiness is to forget oneself, not be preoccupied with oneself. That doesn't mean not feeling one's physical or mental sufferings; the saints themselves passed through these crucifying states. But they did not dwell on them; they continually left these things behind them; when they felt themselves affected by them, they were not surprised, for they knew "they were but dust," as the Psalmist sings; but he also adds: "With God's help, I will be unblemished, and I will guard myself from the depths of sinfulness within me." ...since you allow me to speak to you like a beloved sister, it seems to me that God is asking you for abandonment and unlimited trust during the painful times when you feel those terrible voids. Believe that at those times He is hollowing out in your soul capacities to receive Him, capacities that are, in a way, as infinite as He himself. Try then to will to be wholly joyful under the hand that crucifies you; I would even say that you should look at each suffering, each trial, "as a proof of love" that comes to you directly from God in order to unite you to Him.
>
> Forgetting yourself with respect to your health does not mean neglecting to take care of yourself, for that is your duty and the best of penances, but do it with great abandonment, saying "thank you" to God no matter what happens. When your soul is burdened and fatigued by the weight of your body, do not be discouraged, rather go by faith and love to Him who said: "Come to me and I will refresh you." As for you spirit, never let yourself be depressed by the thought of your sufferings. The great St. Paul says: "Where sin abounds, grace abounds all the more." It seems to me the weakest, even the guiltiest, soul is the one that has the most reason for hope; and the act of forgetting self and throwing oneself into the arms of God glorifies Him and gives Him more joy than all the turning inward and all the self-examinations that make one live with one's own infirmities, though the soul possesses at

its very center a Savior who wants at every moment to purify it.

Do you remember that beautiful passage where Jesus says to His Father "that He has given Him power over all flesh so that He might give eternal life to it"? That is what He wants to do in you: at every moment, He wants you to go out of yourself, to leave all preoccupations, in order to withdraw into the solitude He has chosen for Himself in the depths of your heart. *He* is always there, although you don't feel it; He is waiting for you and wants to establish a "wonderful communion" with you, as we sing in the beautiful liturgy, an intimacy between bride and bridegroom; He, through this continual contact, can deliver you from your weaknesses, your faults, from all that troubles you. Didn't He say: "I have come not to judge but to save." *Nothing* should keep you from going to Him. Don't pay too much attention to whether you are fervent or discouraged; it is the law of our exile to pass from one state to the other like that. Believe that *He* never changes, that in His goodness He is always bending over you to carry you away and keep you safe in Him. If, despite everything, emptiness and sadness overwhelm you, unite this agony with that of the Master in the Garden of Olives, when He said to the Father: "If it is possible, let this cup pass me by." ...it may perhaps seem difficult to forget yourself. Do not worry about it; if you knew how simple it is.... I am going to give you my "secret": think about this God who dwells within you, whose temple you are; Saint Paul speaks like this and we can believe him. Little by little, the soul gets used to living in His sweet company, it understands that it is carrying within it a little Heaven where the God of love has fixed His home. Then it is as if it breathes a divine atmosphere; I would even say that only its body still lives on earth, while the soul lives beyond the clouds and veils, in Him who is the Unchanging One. Do not say that this is not for you, that you are too wretched; on the contrary, that is only one more reason for going to Him who saves. We will be purified, not by looking at this wretchedness, but by looking at Him who is all purity and holiness. Saint Paul says that "He has predestined us to be conformed to His image." In the saddest times, think that the divine artist is using a chisel to make His work more beautiful, and remain at peace beneath the hand that is working on you. (L 249)

It is well worth quoting this remarkable letter in full, if only because of the superb advice it contains. But it also reveals so beautifully Elizabeth's spiritual outlook. It is full of common sense, taking full account of our human weakness and yet at the same time pointing to the heights of holiness. It is completely without self-pity; far from asking "why me?," her utter assurance that she and others are totally loved by God enables her to see purpose and meaning in suffering. But there is no hint of suffering for suffering's sake. Her conversation with Mother Germaine shows the same commonsense approach; if it cannot be avoided, and we have a duty to look after ourselves, then we must use it for his glory. The whole letter is permeated with Scripture, which she meditated upon and lived. Above all, this was no theory, but only what she experienced for herself.

But life was not all suffering. On Wednesday of Holy Week, April 19, Guite gave birth to her second child, Odette. As soon as Easter arrived, Elizabeth wrote to congratulate her sister and tell of her joy at their happiness:

> We have sung the Alleluia, so our Reverend Mother is letting me come tell you right away how united I am with you in your joys of motherhood. I'm so happy to be an aunt once again, and especially of a little girl, for, you see, I think the union that existed between us is going to live on in your sweet home, and I'm delighted that Sabeth has an Odette just as Aunt Elizabeth had a Marguerite. Our dear Mother, who takes such an interest in you, was overjoyed at announcing the big news to me, and she asks me to tell you so. (L 227)

There was also the ordination of André Chevignard to the diaconate on April 8 by Msgr. Maillet, who was in charge of the diocese since Msgr. Le Nordez's resignation. Then on June 29, the feast of St. Peter and St. Paul, he was ordained to the priesthood. The following day he celebrated his first Mass at Carmel.

There were some happy visits from her family, especially from seeing her two nieces. Since the family was not going to Carlipa that year, Elizabeth sent news of the two babies to her Rolland aunts instead:

I'm sorry that Mama, Guite, and her little ones are not with you this summer; those two little darlings would have made you happy. Odette is the best daughter in the world, sweet and quiet like her mother; the parlor visits are so enjoyable when she's along, for she is happy just to look at us with her big eyes without moving. Sabeth is something else; she has to be the center of attention or she is not satisfied. But, on the other hand, when I speak to her about Jesus, she sends Him big kisses that must delight His Heart, for He so loves little ones; she is really very charming, and I believe I have a weakness for her: she is mine! (L 235)

Elizabeth tried to keep going through the long summer months. The doctors thought that with plenty of rest and fresh air she should recover, so Mother Germaine made sure she was out in the garden as much as possible. Her mother was also ill with stomach problems and went away to Switzerland, sorry not to be with Guite and the children and missing them badly. Elizabeth wrote to her August 12:

How that beautiful nature would transport my soul and move it to thanksgiving to the Creator; to think that He has made all that for us!... Our good Mother, who looks after your Sabeth with a truly maternal heart, insists that I spend time out in the fresh air, so, instead of working in our little cell, I'm settled like a hermit in the most deserted part of our big garden, and I spend delightful hours there. All nature seems so full of God to me: the wind blowing in the tall trees, the little birds singing, the beautiful blue sky, everything speaks to me of Him. Oh! Mama, I want you to know my happiness keeps on growing, it takes on infinite proportions, like God Himself, and it is such a calm, sweet happiness; I would like to share my secret with you! Saint Peter, in his first epistle, says: "Because you *believe*, you will be filled with an unshakable joy" (1 Peter 1:8). (L 236)

A few days after she wrote this letter, Mother Germaine relieved her of her duties as turn sister; she never resumed them, though at this time it was meant to be for a month only, to give her extra rest. For Elizabeth, it was a time of even greater solitude and silence, and she looked on it as a sort of retreat. As she carried on with her sewing in the tranquil silence of the garden, she was preoccupied with St. Paul's thoughts on predestination. This was by no means as grim as it sounds. She knew deep down, and despite her doctor's optimism, that she was dying; it was something she had long desired and looked forward to, and it was not something she dreaded. With the deepest fiber of her being, she saw it as simply drawing away the veils that separated her from the full vision of God, veils that were becoming increasingly transparent to her. Heaven had already begun for her, and as she wrote to Framboise at this time, she was comforted by the thought that he who will judge us after death is the one who is living within us, even when we are most wretched, to save and forgive us.

She went on: "Oh, Framboise, how God has enriched us with His gifts; He has predestined us to divine adoption and thus to be heirs of His glorious heritage! 'From all eternity, He chose us in Him that we might be holy in His presence in love,' this is what we are called to be through a 'divine decree'" (L 238).

At the beginning of October, Elizabeth began her private retreat. The evening before, October 8, she wrote to Abbé Chevignard asking for his prayers, setting out her agenda and assuring him of her prayers as he took up his first appointment as curate at Meursault:

> I am setting out this evening on a long journey, nothing less than my private retreat. For ten days, I am going to be in even more absolute solitude, with several extra hours of prayer and our veil lowered whenever I go about the monastery. So you see, your soul sister is going to lead the life of a hermit in the desert; and before burying herself in her Thebaid, she feels a great need to ask for the help of your good prayers, above all for a special intention at the Holy Sacrifice of the Mass. When you consecrate the host in which Jesus, "who alone is the Holy One," is about to become incarnate, would you consecrate me with Him, "as a *sacrifice of praise to His glory*," so all my aspirations, all my impulses, all my actions may be a homage rendered to His Holiness. "Be holy for I am holy"; these are the words I will keep in mind as I enter into recollection; they are the light in whose rays I am going to walk during my divine journey. (L 244)

She had heard this call to holiness, to sanctity, when she first read Thérèse of Lisieux at the age of nineteen. "I desire, in a word, to be a saint," Thérèse had written, and Elizabeth had echoed this in her own act of offering. For her, to be a Carmelite, to be a saint, was the same thing (L 90). For her, as for Thérèse, holiness was simply to love, as she had written to her friend Germaine de Gemeaux a couple of years earlier:

> I commend you to all our saints, and very particularly to our holy Mother Teresa and to Sister Thérèse of the Child Jesus. Yes, my little Germaine, let us live by love, let us be simple like she was, surrendered all the time, immolating ourselves minute by minute by doing God's will without seeking extraordinary things. And then let us make ourselves very little, letting ourselves be carried, like a child in the arms of her mother, by Him who is our All. Yes, my little sister, we are very weak, I would even say we are utterly nothing, but He knows that very well, He so loves to forgive us, to pick us up, then to carry us away in Him, in His purity, in His infinite holiness; that is how He will purify us, through His continual contact with us, through divine touches. He wants us to be so pure, but He Himself will be our purity: we must let ourselves be transformed into one and the same image with Him, and that, quite simply, by loving all the time with the love that establishes unity between those who love each other!
>
> I, too, Germaine, want to be holy, holy to make Him happy. Ask Him to let me live only by love, "it is my vocation." And then let us join in making our days one continual communion: in the morning, let us wake in Love; all day let us surrender ourselves to Love by doing the will of God, in His presence, with Him, in Him, for Him alone. Let us give ourselves all the time in the way He wishes: you by devoting yourself to giving joy to your dear parents. And then when evening comes, after an endless dialogue in our heart, again let us sleep in Love. (L 172)

There was no pride in this determination to aim for the highest holiness. It is what we are created for, and anything less is a misuse of God's love, of the gifts God lavishes on us. Holiness is not of our doing; we give him our weakness, and he gives us his own holiness.

It was no accident that Elizabeth echoed the Great Doxology of the Mass: through him, with him, in him, she saw her life as a continual communion, an offering that was an echo of the Eucharist that is at once thanksgiving and sacrifice. And it was all to the praise of his glory. During this retreat she pondered this phrase of St. Paul's deeply, and shortly after her retreat the community had a "license day" when the sisters could visit each other in their cells. According to Sr. Aimée of Jesus many years later, she mentioned to Elizabeth that she had found this splendid passage in St. Paul, "God has created us for the praise of his glory." Elizabeth went to her cell to look up the Latin text, and it was after this that she took as her "new name, Praise of Glory," or ungrammatically in the Latin, "Laudem Gloriae."

There is obviously a discrepancy here, for Elizabeth, of course, knew the passage well, and it had been growing on her for some time. It could be, though, that it was the Latin text that made it take on new significance for her and made her realize how perfectly it crystallized her inner life. By the end of November, she was writing to Abbé Chevignard again for his name day, the feast of St. Andrew on November 30, and used the Latin text for the first time:

> Help me, Monsieur l'Abbé, I have great need of it, for the more light there is, the more I feel my powerlessness. On December 8th (since you are a high priest), would you consecrate me to the *power of His love* so I may in truth be "Laudem Gloriae"; I read that in Saint Paul and I understood that it was my vocation even now in exile while awaiting the eternal Sanctus. (L 250)

A few days later she wrote to Canon Angles in a similar vein:

> I am going to tell you a very personal secret: my dream is to be "the praise of His glory," I read that in Saint Paul and my Bridegroom made me understand that this was to be my vocation while in exile, waiting to go sing the eternal Sanctus in the City of the saints. But that requires great fidelity, for in order to be a praise of glory, one must be dead to all that is not He, so as to be moved only by His

touch, and the worthless Elizabeth does such foolish things to her Master; but like a tender Father, He forgives her, His divine glance purifies her and, like Saint Paul, she tries "to forget what lies behind and press on toward what is ahead" (Phil. 3:13). (L 256)

In the Scriptures the name of a person has profound meaning; the name of a person is what they are. There are many examples of God giving a new name to a person, thereby changing them deeply and signifying a new calling, new responsibilities, and at the same time giving them the gifts they need to fulfill that calling: Simon to Peter, Abram to Abraham, Jacob to Israel. Her new name was just as significant for Elizabeth, a profound grace and gift from God, and it came as she started the final, agonizing stage of her climb to Calvary.

12

THE FELLOWSHIP OF HIS SUFFERINGS

On Christmas Eve Elizabeth was helping the other novices to prepare the crib, and one of them heard her murmuring, "My little King of Love; we'll be very much closer to each other next year!"

"How do you know that?" her companion asked, startled. Elizabeth looked at her, gave her usual radiant smile and said nothing (Souv. 170).

Her meaning was underlined on New Year's Day when it was the custom for the sisters to draw tickets with the name of their patron saint for the year on it. Elizabeth was delighted to draw St. Joseph, patron of a happy death. "He's coming to take me to the Father," she exclaimed and dismissed with a slight gesture the laughing and somewhat alarmed denials of her sisters (Souv. 173).

On the feast of the Epiphany Guite again made them the Kings' cake, and Elizabeth gave her little niece Sabeth a doll dressed as a Carmelite, exact in every detail. Sabeth was delighted with it and called it "Tata," probably the nearest she could get to "tante" (aunt). Guite gave Elizabeth another warm underskirt to replace her old one that was worn and threadbare. Elizabeth needed all the warmth she could get against the bitter cold. Guite came to see her toward the end of January but had to leave the two children, who both had colds, at home. "The temperature in the parlors of Carmel," Elizabeth remarked to Mme. Angles, "would hardly be good for colds" (L 264). She herself had to keep apologizing in her letters for her poor handwriting due to the cold and her chilblains; she didn't mention that her utter exhaustion also made it almost impossible to hold a pen.

It was now three years since her profession, and she normally would have moved out of the novitiate into the community as a full chapter sister. Mother Germaine, though, asked her to stay in the novitiate to help with the young sisters.

During the second half of January there was a community retreat preached by Abbé Rolland, S.J., and then Lent was soon upon them. In the novitiate Elizabeth listened to the novices making plans for Lent but did not feel drawn to any of their schemes for meditating on the Lord's Passion.

After the midday recreation, therefore, she went to her cell and opened her copy of the Scriptures at her favorite place, the letters of St. Paul. Opened at random, her eyes fell on the text: "That I may know him...and the fellowship of his sufferings, being made conformable to his death" (Phil. 3:10). Paul was telling her that her Lent was not simply to contemplate her Lord's sufferings but to share in them.

In the middle of Lent her health became worse. Mother Germaine was already making her rest as much as possible, and her family was sending ice and other foods that were easy to swallow so she might be able to eat. Then, a few days after St. Joseph's Day, March 19, her health declined to such an extent that she was transferred from the cell she loved so much and installed permanently in the infirmary. "I knew St. Joseph would come for me this year," Elizabeth exclaimed happily, "and he's here already" (Souv. 178).

The community, realizing that they might very well lose the young sister they loved so dearly, began a real crusade of prayer for her recovery. They started novenas to Margaret of Beaune, a Carmelite nun who lived in the seventeenth century, and whose process of beatification had begun in Rome. But the answer to their prayers was to make it apparent that Elizabeth was to follow their older sister along the path of suffering. On the evening of Palm Sunday, she had such a severe fainting fit that the community thought she was dying and sent for the parish priest, Abbé Donin, to give her the last sacraments. With the rapid swings that characterized her illness, she had recovered from the worst effects by the time Abbé Donin arrived, although she was in severe pain.

Elizabeth herself was radiantly happy despite her suffering, feeling that the thin veil that separated her from her Master was soon to be torn aside. The parish priest quickly realized that the usual exhortations to the dying were superfluous in Elizabeth's case: she was only too impatient for that longed-for moment. After her death he wrote to Mme. Catez:

> I consider this brief meeting with her to have been one of the greatest graces of my priestly life. It is a precious and unforgettable memory, a vivid and very profound impression for which words are totally inadequate. I can only say that if in the course of my ministry I have sometimes seen "those veils drawn back that hide from the dying the splendors of eternity," to give some glimpse of them; if I have sometimes seen the dying transfigured, some haloed light upon their faces, a radiance not of this world—never has it been more visible than that night when I went in to your dear daughter's cell to give the last Sacraments. Despite her intense suffering she was calm and smiling, her hands joined in prayer...." (Souv. 446ff)

"If I were younger I would become a religious," remarked Abbé Donin as he left the enclosure afterward, "dying is so beautiful in Carmel" (Souv. 180). During the days of Holy Week, Mother Germaine rarely left Elizabeth's bedside. She was very weak and in great pain, although she later wrote of them: "What ineffable days I spent expecting the great vision...in my desire to go to Him" (L 278).

Not wanting to upset her family, especially as her mother was not at all well, Elizabeth had kept from them how seriously ill she really was. Although Mme. Catez knew Elizabeth was not well, she didn't know exactly how ill. During Lent, as her health deteriorated alarmingly, no one had dared to tell her mother the truth. But now Mother Germaine realized that since Elizabeth had nearly died, they could keep it from her mother no longer. On the Monday of Holy Week she told Mme. Catez the truth. It was a terrible blow, but so often we tend to underestimate another's strength and courage. Elizabeth was too weak to come to the parlor, so Mme. Catez wrote to her, a letter Elizabeth cherished and read over and over again. It revealed just how far her mother, too, had journeyed in her union with God and acceptance of his will, however anguished she might have been. It was a tremendous comfort to Elizabeth, for however happy she herself was at the prospect of being with the Lord she loved so much, she was deeply aware of how painful it would be for her family. Yet again, she was having to come to terms with the fact that she was going to cause suffering to those closest to her, and whom she loved so dearly.

But God was not asking this sacrifice of them just yet. On Good Friday she again suffered a relapse, but during the night there was a slight change for the better; when her infirmarians came to her the following morning, they found her kneeling on the bed. She was even able to eat a little and asked if she could go to the choir for the Easter liturgy. This, of course, was out of the question, but the sisters were able to sing their Easter alleluias with much greater joy than they expected at this slight improvement. Mme. Catez, too, was able to thank God that her daughter had been spared for a time, as she knelt in the chapel that Easter.

Elizabeth had dictated a letter to her mother during Holy Week, which Mother Germaine wrote out for her, but she was just strong enough, the following week, to write a letter herself in pencil, in small, feeble writing. Knowing how worried her mother was about Carmelite austerity, she was always at pains to reassure her how well and lovingly she was being looked after:

> I know you're ill, and my good Mother here, who is constantly at the bedside of her little child, keeps me posted about *your dear health*. You can't imagine the care she lavishes on me, with all the tenderness and delicacy of a mother's heart! If you knew how happy I am in the solitude of my little infirmary; my Master is here with me, and we live night and day in a sweet heart-to-heart. I appreciate the happiness of being a Carmelite even more, and I pray to God for the little Mama who gave me to Him. I've been drawn still closer to Heaven since this illness; I'll tell you all about it one day. Oh, little Mama, let us prepare for our eternity, let us live with Him, for He alone can accompany and help us on this great journey. He is a God of love; we cannot comprehend the extent to which He loves us, *above all when He sends us trials.* (L 267)

For the first time she signed her letter "Sabeth," dropping her name in religion to try and bridge in some little way the separation imposed by Carmelite enclosure between her mother and herself. She fully expected to die at any moment and at the end of April. She wrote to her sister a letter that in its solemn tones reads like a last will and testament:

I don't know if the hour has come to pass from this world to my Father, for I am much better and the little saint of Beaune seems to want to cure me. But, you see, at times it seems to me that the Divine Eagle wants to swoop down on His little prey and carry her off to where He is: into dazzling light! You have always put your Sabeth's happiness before your own, and I am sure that if I fly away, you will rejoice over my first meeting with Divine Beauty. When the veil is lifted, how happy I will be to disappear into the secret of His Face, and that is where I will spend my eternity, in the bosom of the Trinity that was already my dwelling place here below. Just think, my Guite! to contemplate in His light the splendors of the Divine Being, to search into all the depths of His mystery, to become one with Him whom we love, to sing unceasingly of His glory and His love, to be like Him because we see Him as He is!

Little sister, I would be happy to go up above to be your Angel. How jealous I would be for the beauty of your soul that I have loved so much already here on earth! I leave you my devotion for the Three, to "Love." Live within Them in the heaven of your soul; the Father will overshadow you, placing something like a cloud between you and the things of this earth to keep you all His. He will communicate His power to you so you can love Him with a love as strong as death; the Word will imprint in your soul, as in a crystal, the image of His own beauty, so you may be pure with His purity, luminous with His light; the Holy Spirit will transform you into a mysterious lyre, which, in silence, beneath His divine touch, will produce a magnificent canticle to Love; then you will be "the praise of His glory" I dreamed of being on earth. You will take my place; I will be "Laudem Gloriae" before the throne of the Lamb, and you, "Laudem Gloriae" in the center of your soul; we will always be united, little sister.

> Always believe in Love. If you have to suffer, think that
> you are even *more loved*, and always sing in thanksgiv-
> ing. He is so jealous for the beauty of your soul.... That is
> all He has in view. (L 269)

In the letter to her mother, Elizabeth spoke about telling her mother "all about it soon." This was a reference to plans Mother Germaine was making for bringing her down to the parlor in her bed for what the community fully expected to be her last visit with her family. This visit took place early in May. She also arranged for a photograph to be taken of Elizabeth in the infirmary as a last keepsake for them. Even in the photograph, some idea of the radiance shining out in her can be seen as she lies on the bed, her eyes wide and beautiful, a lovely smile transfiguring her face. Above the bed was propped a framed painting of the Annunciation, sent to her the previous November by Mme. de Sourdon.

Elizabeth could not write a "last will and testament letter" to her mother as she had for her sister, though, for this would have been too painful. Neither could Mother Germaine bring herself to tell Mme. Catez the full, harrowing details of her daughter's illness; it would only have added to her worries, without her being able to do anything about it.

Mother Germaine felt, however, that she needed to confide in someone close to the family whose discretion she could trust. She therefore held back a letter of Elizabeth's, written May 9 to Canon Angles, to include a letter of her own. It was written after Elizabeth had suffered another severe relapse May 13, from four in the morning until two o'clock the following day, when they again thought she was dying:

> Since then, what sufferings throughout this poor body!
> Her mother does not know the whole truth of her crucify-
> ing condition; her heart is broken enough already, I tell
> her only what is necessary to keep her in her present
> admirable disposition of abandonment and submission
> to God's will. But to you, dear Monsieur le Chanoine, I
> can confide that our Elizabeth reminds us of the Divine

Master on the Cross. She is in a lot of pain from little
afflictions added to her general condition—the sense of
a fire consuming her inside, and thus a scorching thirst
that cannot be quenched because the least drop of water
causes very acute suffering in that poor stomach, which is
incapable of receiving any nourishment and *very* painful.... But in the midst of all that, what peace, what beautiful serenity! She suffers as she has lived, like a saint."
(L 271, n. 1)

For Elizabeth herself, the consuming fire and the burning thirst of
her physical condition was also a description of the love that burned
within her; indeed, for her there was little difference. Just as she had
accepted the sacrifices of ordinary life as God's tokens of love, now
she looked beyond her present appalling suffering to the spiritual di-
mension within and beyond it. She saw it as allowed by God, calling
it Love's sickness, his means of drawing her closer to himself and
conforming her to the likeness of his beloved, crucified Son, which
was her ambition.

If God was asking great things of her, he was also giving her the
grace to bear them. Mother Germaine came in to see her on the feast
of the Ascension, May 24, a little later than usual, since she always
tried to make her thanksgiving after Mass and Communion by
Elizabeth's bedside when Elizabeth was unable to receive Communion herself. It was a heavy sacrifice that her inability to swallow prevented her from receiving Communion, and that she was too weak
even to go to the infirmary grille, since at that time the priest did not
have permission to come inside the enclosure to bring holy Communion to the sick; the previous December Pope Plus X had issued an
encyclical permitting and encouraging daily Communion. This day,
though, she found Elizabeth radiant with joy as she brushed aside the
prioress's apologies:

O Mother, don't worry about me. The good God has given
me such grace that I lost all track of time. This morning he
spoke this word deep within me: "If anyone loves me, my
Father will love them; we will come to them and make our
home within them." At that very moment I experienced

the truth of it. I cannot describe how the three divine Persons revealed themselves, but I saw them holding loving
converse within me and I still seem to see them. How great
God is and how he loves us. (Souv. 217)

It no longer seemed such an enormous sacrifice to be deprived of
Holy Communion after that. Her "Three" were within her, and she
would sink into profound prayer to be there with them. Her health
began to improve very slightly after this, though. As soon as she was
able to swallow a little she went to Holy Communion when she could.
Still too weak to walk, one of her infirmarians, Marie of the Holy
Spirit, would lift her in her strong arms and carry her to the communion grille in the infirmary chapel. By the beginning of June, Elizabeth
was strong enough to be carried on a chaise longue to the tribune of
the infirmary so she could hear Mass. Abbé Donin, the parish priest,
on the occasions when he came to say Mass for them, recalled how,
no matter how weak she was, she seemed to have a brief surge of
energy as she came to the grille, as if her longing to receive her Lord
gave her that little bit of extra strength.

As she was now able to eat a little, her friends and family vied
with each other in sending her things that they thought she might be
able to manage. She had to tell her mother that the cake she was sending was too much for her "troublesome stomach," and that she pre-
ferred white cheese. She was also able to swallow the mildest Swiss
chocolate, such as Suchard. The cook, Sr. Martha of Jesus, whom
Elizabeth called her "mother," was also untiring in her efforts to provide her with things she might be able to eat. She "was so affectionate
and delicate in her gratitude for the least service one gave her that it
was a joy to go to her," Sr. Martha recalled (L 281, n. 1).

Since Elizabeth was a little stronger, Mother Germaine arranged
for her mother to come and see her every day for a fortnight at the end
of May, which was a joy for them both. It was just one of the many
little thoughtful things the community did for her and which often
made her exclaim, "What a Carmel!"

Mme. Catez then went away to Saint-Sulpice at the beginning of
June to attend a triduum, a three-day celebration held in honor of the

beatification of the Carmelite martyrs of Compiègne, who were sent to the guillotine during the French Revolution. She then stayed on in Paris with the Hallo family for a prolonged visit and a rest. The Hallos were wonderfully supportive of Mme. Catez and Guite at this time and kept Elizabeth informed of her mother's health, which was improving a little. Elizabeth, too, was able to reassure her mother that her appetite was also improving, that she could eat white cheese and Bruges bread, as well as the ice and Suchard chocolate, which she ate in small amounts during the day.

On June 12 Guite came for a visit with the two children, and on June 15 the community celebrated Mother Germaine's feast day. Elizabeth had collaborated with another sister, whom she called "my sister of the Child Jesus." This was another sister of the white veil, Anne-Marie of the Child Jesus; she was thirty-three at this time, and although she was not sleeping in the infirmary, she was often in and out with bouts of ill health. Anne-Marie was convinced that she, too, was dying, but actually lived to the age of seventy-one.

Elizabeth called her "her soul sister," but two people more unalike in character would have been hard to find. Anne-Marie was childlike and naive, easily swayed and emotional, and inclined to religious experiences that were the product of her vivid imagination. Elizabeth, with her loving nature, took her under her wing while they were in the infirmary together and gently encouraged her along the path of genuine faith, love, and self-giving.

Together they prepared a small display of cards and gifts for Mother Germaine's feast day with help from Guite and the Hallo family and also composed some poems. Mme. Catez and Mme. Hallo sent gifts from Paris: booklets on the Carmelites of Compiègne, a translation of the Psalms, maxims of St. John of the Cross, and at Mother Germaine's request, a book of Ruysbroeck's works, which Elizabeth was to read avidly in the months ahead.

For the first time since she had moved into the infirmary, Elizabeth was strong enough to be able to be with the whole community for the feast day; until then she had only been able to have one sister at a time visit her. They moved her bed into the chapter room that was next to the infirmary, and where they all gathered for the festivities.

It was a welcomed break in what could be the tedium of life in the infirmary, when she was not well enough to do very much and was obviously more secluded than being in community. She was not alone in the infirmary, though. Her infirmarian was Anne of Jesus, helped by Marie of the Holy Spirit, who had been in the novitiate with Elizabeth for a short while; they were with her a good deal of the time. The older sister of the white veil, Marie of the Incarnation, whom she called her "grandmama," was also permanently in the infirmary, as well as Anne-Marie of the Child Jesus. The small items of handiwork and embroidery Elizabeth made during her final illness are still lovingly preserved.

Mme. Catez arrived back in Dijon on June 22 and came round to Carmel the following day. Elizabeth was relieved to see her looking much better after her holiday with the Hallos, and she herself, although still confined to bed, was a little stronger. Her mother, though, returned from Paris worried about the political situation. In the July of the previous year the new government under Sarrien passed a new bill of separation of church and state, which had become law on December 11, 1905. The Vatican had protested strongly, and when government agents moved in to take the inventories of church property required under the law, there were ugly clashes in some parts of the country in which at least one person was killed. Mother Germaine had given some of the statues belonging to the community into Guite's safekeeping until things had quieted down. One advantage under the new law of separation, however, was that the chapel was allowed to reopen to the public that June. They were able to celebrate the feast of Corpus Christi publicly for the first time in three years.

Mme. Catez was worried, though, that the community might still be forced to leave France. Elizabeth was able to reassure her mother that should this happen, she herself would not leave but would return to her mother's house. As far as Elizabeth was concerned, her dearest wish was that she should live and die in the Carmel she loved so much, and where she was deeply happy. Some of this happiness is reflected in a letter she wrote to her friend Cécile Lignon, recalling the good times they had together:

> [Your letter] came to visit me in the solitude of the infirmary where I have been for three months. I really thought I was going to fly away to Heaven. Death is so sweet for a Carmelite that its perspective gave me only joy, and I knew it would not take me away from those I love any more than the dear grilles that hide me have separated me from them. You know that in my heart I am always your little mama, and if I had gone to Heaven, I would have been so even more. Sometimes people think that those inside the cloister are no longer able to love, but it is just the contrary, and for my part I have never had more affection. It seems to me that my heart has expanded, and my dear Cécile holds a very big place there, as well as her little mama by whom I have always felt so loved! Oh, how I think of those nice vacations at Saint-Hilaire; I have not forgotten anything, not even the "four-step" danced by my Cécile! I am writing to you on my little bed, for I no longer have the strength to get up. If you saw how well I am cared for…. Our Reverend Mother is a true mama to me, she showers me with kindness just as a mother would shower her little child. Oh, my little Cécile, how happy I am in my Carmel; it seems to me one cannot have more happiness except in Heaven, and this happiness is like a prelude, since God alone is already the Object of it. But, just as in Heaven, they do not forget those on earth; your Elizabeth thinks of those she has left and prays for them. (L 290)

13

THE ROAD TO CALVARY HAS OPENED

On February 25 that year, Pope Pius X consecrated fourteen new bishops, among them Pierre Dadolle, the new bishop of Dijon. He took possession of his diocese March 15, and signaled his intention to visit Carmel for the feast day of Our Lady of Mount Carmel, July 16. Before Guite and her family set off for Sainte-Marie-sur-Ouche for their holidays, Elizabeth wrote to ask her to return the statues in her safe keeping so that they would be in place for the bishop's visit. With the family was Clémence Blanc, a postulant who had just left Carmel and was staying with them for a while. Elizabeth had been her "angel" for a while, and she wrote affectionately to her "dear little Tobias."

Elizabeth, still confined to bed, also wrote a long letter to Canon Angles, revealing some of her inner life to him, as well as news of her family:

> I love the thought by Saint Paul you sent me! It seems to me it is being realized in me, on this little bed that is the altar on which I am being immolated to Love. Oh, ask that my likeness to the adored Image might be more perfect each day: "Configuratus morti ejus." That is what haunts me, what gives strength to my soul in suffering. If you knew what a work of destruction I feel throughout my whole being; the road to Calvary has opened, and I am quite joyful to walk it like a bride beside the divine Cruci-fied. I will be twenty-six on the 18th; I do not know if this year will end in time or eternity, and I ask you, like a child of her father, to please consecrate me at Holy Mass as a sacrifice of praise to the glory of God. Oh, consecrate me so completely that I may be no longer *myself but Him*, so the Father, in looking at me, may recognize Him; so "I might be like Him in His death," so I may suffer in myself

what is wanting in His passion for His body, the Church, and then bathe me in the Blood of Christ so I may be strong with His strength; I feel so little, so weak.... A Dieu, dear Monsieur le Chanoine. I saw my good Mama last week; she seems very tired; she worries; the doctor told Guite she is getting much weaker. I am sharing all this with you so you might bear it with God. (L 294)

Elizabeth was being torn two ways. She felt her path was that of Calvary, but the sisters were praying hard for her recovery. Mother Germaine told her that if she was really grateful to be in Carmel, she should pray to be made well so that she could work in the community once again. But at one point, as she dutifully prayed to be cured, she heard a voice deep inside her saying, "Earthly offices are no longer for you." Filled with a deep peace and joy, she gave up praying for a cure and set her sights once more on the heaven for which she was so homesick.

Mother Germaine came to see her one day early in July; Elizabeth was feeling so exhausted that she said she felt as if she was dying. "Instead of talking like that," replied the prioress, "you should think about trying to walk again" (Souv. 206).

After she had left, Elizabeth prayed hard to Thérèse of Lisieux—not for a cure, for she knew Thérèse understood her longing for heaven, having shared it herself—but that she might be able to walk once more. Although she hadn't been able even to sit up in bed before, she now managed to sit on the edge of the bed. By July 11 she wrote to her mother that she was able to walk:

You'd really laugh if you saw me like a little old lady bent over my stick. Our good Mother takes me by the arm onto the terrace; I'm quite proud of my comings and goings; I'm longing to give you a demonstration; you'd surely get a good laugh, for I'm very funny, and I'm delighted to announce this good news to you, knowing it will make you very happy. Don't cry over your Sabeth; God will leave her with you a little while longer. (L 295)

By mid-July she was even able to dispense with her stick and went to the parlor without it to see her mother the Sunday after her birthday. Although there was no other improvement in her health, being able to walk made a big difference. In the early hours of the morning, the infirmarians would put a chair out on the terrace for her, so that after long, sleepless nights she could sit in the welcomed coolness of the morning air and rest her head, racked by almost constant, blinding headaches. As soon as she was seated, she would close her eyes and almost at once be lost in her habitual, profound prayer.

Beside her chair was a small table on which she kept a few books: John of the Cross, Angela of Foligno, and Ruysbroeck. She also took with her everywhere a small statue of Our Lady of Lourdes that she had had in her bedroom at home and had asked her mother for now. When the pain was almost too much for her to bear, she would take refuge in the dim silence of the small infirmary tribune overlooking the sanctuary, where she could pray before the Blessed Sacrament. She would place Janua Coeli, Gate of Heaven, as she called the statue, at the entrance, often the only sign that she was there as she sat huddled on the floor, bent double with pain.

Mother Germaine found her there one day; her eyes were tearful, but she managed to smile and said, "I came to take refuge in my Master's prayer, I need his divine strength; I'm in such pain" (Souv. 210).

Among her family and friends, and in the wider circle outside Carmel, there was concern that she wasn't receiving all the medical help she needed. This was one reason Elizabeth kept stressing in her letters how well she was being looked after. Guite's husband Georges, especially was becoming increasingly angry at what he considered Carmel's neglect of real medical treatment, however lovingly she was being cared for, however well-meaning the community was. "One doesn't let a young girl of twenty-six die like that without helping her" (JTD v. 1b, p. 351), his sister Madeleine remembers him storming. He felt she should be in a hospital. In fact, as early as her first collapse in May, the doctors attending her had considered the possibility of an operation and had then decided against it.

Toward the end of July, therefore, Georges came to see the prioress and afterward spoke to Elizabeth herself. The community's regular doctor was Dr. Barbier, but now Georges arranged for two others, Drs. Morlot and Gautrelet, to examine her. Aware of the criticism that was flying around, Elizabeth told her mother she received Dr. Gautrelet as warmly as possible so he wouldn't go away with a bad impression of Carmel. She added:

> I love my Carmel so much, I want all who come near me
> to share my feelings. He stayed a long time, but I don't
> think he's the one who will bring me back to life; do you
> know what he advised me to take so my stomach would
> recover: a good stew with bacon; I'll bet you have about
> as much of an appetite for that as I do! I did try to take a
> few spoonfuls more, and that upset my stomach, increased
> my vomiting and so forth; so I'm back to taking my little
> spoonful and that's all I can do. (L 305)

Understandably, the doctors also decided to try a stomach pump; the effect on her ulcerated stomach was sheer torture and was almost too much even for Elizabeth's considerable courage. "I have often longed for martyrdom," she remarked. "I don't anymore, but I prepare myself for these painful sessions in that spirit" (Souv. 223). They further weakened her already exhausted body and shattered her nervous system. She dreaded these sessions but would simply kiss her crucifix and allowed them to carry out the procedure with her usual serenity.

However well-meaning Georges's intentions were in trying to provide more medical care for his sister-in-law, the only result they had was to give her even more pain and discomfort. Carmel's lavish care and love were far better after all; stomach pumps and bacon were no remedy, and there was, after all, no cure.

Elizabeth herself didn't see the point of medication and was unconcerned that at this time she was not even given painkillers. If anyone tried to ease her pain she would simply reply, "It's not worth it, I have almost completed my journey. God has made me understand that before I see him face to face soon, far from taking my ease, Laudem Gloriae has to extract as much prayer and suffering from herself as possible" (Souv. 223).

She was far more concerned about her mother's continuing ill-health, which was undoubtedly made worse by her anxiety about her daughter. Elizabeth did all she could to reassure her that she was being well looked after and that Mother Germaine was giving her genuine motherly care; she encouraged her mother to look after herself, to let Guite give her a good spoiling, and to let herself rest quietly in the arms of God, as she herself was doing. "It's so simple, this intimacy with God; it gives rest rather than tires—like a child rests beneath the watchful eyes of its mother" (L 301).

At the end of July, Mother Marie of Jesus arrived in Dijon on business connected with the Paray-le-Monial foundation. The tiny property on the Ruelle du Loup had only been meant as a temporary measure, and they had purchased a piece of land on the top of a hill just outside Paray with a wide, peaceful view of meadows, trees, bushes, and a stream winding through. The monastery was built as gradually as funds allowed, and the community finally moved into their new, more spacious home in May 1906. This visit was to be Mother Marie of Jesus' final visit to her old community and a great joy for them all, but especially for Elizabeth. The prioress who had first introduced her to Carmel could see for herself the manifest holiness that was shining from her now. Unable to sleep one night because of the heat, Mother Marie of Jesus sat up until about one in the morning, praying for the community she had left behind in Paray. The following day she wrote to them:

> I have had a beautiful sermon coming into contact with Sister Elizabeth of the Trinity. The little sister is a real saint: she speaks of her approaching death with a lovely simplicity, a joyous serenity and peace, and lives in the anticipation of seeing God, in perfect surrender and love. She seems to be already in the retreat of eternity. (*A Carmelite of the Sacred Heart*, 144)

A few days later Mother Marie of Jesus returned to Paray-le-Monial, and on August 14 Elizabeth wrote to her for the feast of the Assumption the following day:

> Laudem gloriae is coming to sing very close to your soul on the eve of your feast day. On her lyre is always the hymn of silence, is that not the most beautiful of canticles, the one sung in the bosom of the Three? ...My Mother, I enclose myself in this sacred silence of the Holy Trinity so I can better celebrate your feast.... Beatitude attracts me more and more; between my Master and me that is all we talk about, and His whole work is to prepare me for eternal life. (L 306)

A couple of weeks earlier, August 2, as she looked back with grateful affection on the day she had entered Carmel five short years before, she wrote to her mother:

> I was recalling that last evening, and as I wasn't able to sleep, I settled myself close to my window and stayed there until almost midnight, in prayer with my Master. I spent a heavenly evening; the sky was so blue, so calm, you could feel such a silence in the monastery; and I went back over these five years, so filled with graces. Oh, little Mama whom I love, don't regret the happiness you have given me. (L 302)

The last photograph of Elizabeth, taken about a month before her death.

14

FROM THE PALACE OF PAIN AND BLISS

During these final months of her illness, Mother Germaine lifted all restrictions on the number of letters Elizabeth was allowed to write, the only restriction being when it might tire her too much. These letters were valuable to her because in them she could share her inner life freely with those to whom she was writing. But she was also feeling the need to put her teaching into a more systematic form than letter writing would allow, and at the beginning of August, Elizabeth asked Mother Germaine if she could write a small treatise, which was later entitled "Heaven in Faith."

She intended it as a "surprise" for Guite, a small memento, but in fact Guite only received it some two months after her sister's death, as Mother Germaine kept it for reference while she was writing her account of Elizabeth's life.

She wrote it in a small notebook bound in black oilcloth with almost no alterations. She planned it along the lines of the Carmelite ten-day retreat, each day having two parts, corresponding with the two set prayer times of a Carmelite day. Each meditation started with a quotation from Scripture. Elizabeth drew not only on the Scriptures but also on her favorite authors whose books she kept by her: John of the Cross, Teresa of Avila, Thérèse of Lisieux, Angela of Foligno, and Ruysbroeck.

Her use of all these writers did not mean she was recycling other people's ideas; it was, rather, an example of her "passion for listening," as she called it. She had absorbed their thoughts, because they expressed her own thought, but she made them entirely her own, weaving them into her own special gift of expression that came from the depths of her lived experience.

It is well to remember that she intended this small booklet for her sister, a married woman with children. She spoke from her experience as a nun but had no doubt at all that what she wanted to pass on to her sister would have just as much relevance to one "living in the world," for it sprang from the Gospels and Jesus' invitation to everyone to live in union with him. The object of the "retreat," she said, "is to make us more like our adored Master, and even more, to become so one with Him that we may say: 'I live no longer I, but He lives in me'" (HF 28).

The theme of the retreat is expressed in the very first lines, the passage from John 17:24: "Father, I will that where I am, they also may be whom you have given me," and Elizabeth followed that through with her own inexorable logic: "He wills that where he is we should be also, not only for eternity, but already in time, which is eternity begun and still in progress" (HF 1).

Elizabeth then develops the implications of this in her short meditations. If God, the "Three"—Father, Son, and Holy Spirit—wants us to be with him, then that is where we have to remain, not for a few moments or a few hours, but permanently, habitually. "Remain in Me, pray in Me, adore in Me, love in Me, suffer in Me, work and act in Me" (HF 3).

And God is not far away, he is in us; so to be with him we have to enter into the deep center of our being where he is, and it is love that takes us there. Love not only takes us there, but we find love, God's love for us, which we are impelled to return. This is not always easy, for self gets in the way; in the light of his love for us, we see so clearly our own weakness and poverty, but then his love for us is the consuming fire that will gradually burn away the dross. His love then becomes ours, enabling us to love as he does, which enlarges our capacity to receive his life.

This can be at once a painful and a blissful process. "He asks for more than we of ourselves are capable of giving" (HF 18). He will never be satisfied by anything less than the whole of ourselves, but his generosity is never outdone: "All that He has, all that He is, He gives; all that we have, all that we are, He takes away" (HF 18). That is, he takes away our poverty, our weakness, and gives us his life, but we do so cling to our rags. As his life flows over us and into us, though, as we come to believe in the love God has for us, our faith is awakened; it simplifies us within, making us single-hearted in our love.

It returns us to the image God has of us from all eternity, which is ourselves in his own image and likeness, set free and purified of sin; he clothes us with his own life, which is our holiness. This is what God has created us for, what his plan is for us.

But this also means being like Christ crucified, imitating the one who was "made humbler yet." As we do, we find God, for "it seems to me that to be plunged into humility is to be plunged into God" (HF 37). The one who most closely realized this ideal of union with God was Mary.

Elizabeth probably ended her "retreat" just before the feast of the Assumption, and the first half of the tenth day is a hymn to her:

> "If you knew the gift of God...." There is one who knew this gift of God, one who did not lose one particle of it, one who was so pure, so luminous that she seemed to be the Light itself: "Speculum justitiae [Mirror of justice]." One whose life was so simple, so lost in God that there is hardly anything we can say about it. "Virgo Fidelis": that is, Faithful Virgin, "who kept all these things in her heart." She remained so little, so recollected in God's presence, in the seclusion of the temple, that she drew down upon herself the delight of the Holy Trinity: "Because He has looked upon the lowliness of His servant, henceforth all generations shall call me blessed!" The Father bending down to this beautiful creature, who was so unaware of her own beauty, willed that she be the Mother in time of Him whose Father He is in eternity. Then the Spirit of love who presides over all of God's works came upon her; the Virgin said her *fiat*: "Behold the servant of the Lord, be it done to me according to Your word," and the greatest of mysteries was accomplished. By the descent of the Word in her, Mary became forever God's prey. (HF 39)

Elizabeth could see in Mary what life in Christ meant, of what her
own calling as a contemplative involved. Mary was one who responded
perfectly to what God asked of her. In other words, she was the perfect "Praise of Glory," the ideal to which Elizabeth herself aspired.
She therefore ended her "retreat" with a vibrant hymn that spelled out
in greater detail what she saw that ideal to be:

> How do we realize this great dream of the Heart of our
> God, this immutable will for our souls? In a word, how do
> we correspond to our vocation and become perfect
> *Praises of Glory* of the Most Holy Trinity?
>
> "In Heaven" each soul is a praise of glory of the Fa-
> ther, the Word, and the Holy Spirit, for each soul is estab-
> lished in pure love and "lives no longer its own life, but
> the life of God." Then it knows Him, St. Paul says, as it is
> known by Him. In other words "its intellect is the intel-
> lect of God, its will the will of God, its love the very love
> of God. In reality it is the Spirit of love and of strength
> who transforms the soul, for to Him it has been given to
> supply what is lacking to the soul," as St. Paul says again.
>
> A praise of glory is a soul that lives in God, that loves
> Him with a pure and disinterested love, without seeking
> itself in the sweetness of this love; that loves Him beyond
> all His gifts and even though it would not have received
> anything from Him, it desires the good of the Object thus
> loved. Now how do we *effectively* desire and will good to
> God if not in accomplishing His will since this will orders
> everything for His greater glory? Thus the soul must sur-
> render itself to this will completely, passionately, so as to
> will nothing else but what God wills.
>
> A praise of glory is a soul of silence that remains like
> a lyre under the mysterious touch of the Holy Spirit so that
> He may draw from it divine harmonies; it knows that suf-
> fering is a string that produces still more beautiful sounds;
> so it loves to see this string on its instrument that it may
> more delightfully move the Heart of its God.
>
> A praise of glory is a soul that gazes on God in faith
> and simplicity; it is a reflector of all that He is; it is like a
> bottomless abyss into which He can flow and expand; it is
> also like a crystal through which He can radiate and con-
> template all His perfections and His own splendor. A soul
> which thus permits the divine Being to satisfy in itself His

need to communicate "all that He is and all that He has," is in reality the praise of glory of all His gifts.

Finally, a praise of glory is one who is always giving thanks. Each of her acts, her movements, her thoughts, her aspirations, at the same time that they are rooting her more deeply in love, are like an echo of the eternal Sanctus.

In the Heaven of glory the blessed have no rest "day or night, saying: Holy, holy, holy is the Lord God Almighty.... They fall down and worship Him who lives forever and ever...."

In the heaven of her soul, the praise of glory has already begun her work of eternity. Her song is uninterrupted, for she is under the action of the Holy Spirit who effects everything in her; and although she is not always aware of it, for the weakness of nature does not allow her to be established in God without distractions, she always sings, she always adores, for she has, so to speak, wholly passed into praise and love in her passion for the glory of her God. In the heaven of our soul let us be praises of glory of the Holy Trinity, praises of love of our Immaculate Mother. One day the veil will fall, we will be introduced into the eternal courts, and there we will sing in the bosom of infinite Love. And God will give us "the new name promised to the Victor." What will it be? LAUDEM GLORIAE. (HF 41–44)

Elizabeth handed the small notebook to her prioress and then began what they both knew would be her last real retreat from August 16 to 31. Mother Germaine said it would be her "novitiate for heaven," a thought Elizabeth loved. She was not able to observe it with the same degree of solitude she had before she became ill. In the infirmary there were regular visits from her doctors, and her two infirmarians were at hand to look after her. She spent much of her time outside on the terrace, as well as her visits to the infirmary tribune. She agreed with Mother Germaine not to let her family know she was in retreat, so they would still be free to visit her.

Mother Germaine suggested that she keep another notebook in which to jot down her thoughts during the retreat; the prioress was looking ahead to the time when she would have to write Elizabeth's obituary notice, which would be sent round to the other Carmels.

Elizabeth understood and smilingly agreed. Once more she took a small black notebook and, during the long, sleepless nights, when she was free of interruption, she wrote her "Last Retreat."

Written by the light of her little oil lamp, the "Last Retreat" bears physical witness to the intensity of her suffering. She managed to write it in ink, but it had many corrections, erasures, and additions as she tried to get her exhausted mind to concentrate. She wrote it through a haze of such violent pain that she often thought she would faint from it. But this does not appear in what she wrote, which is lucid and serene, flowing from a self-control she described in her "Last Retreat" on the second day:

> "My soul is always in my hands." My Master sang this in His soul, and that is why in the midst of all His anguish He always remained the calm and strong One. My soul is always in my hands! What does that mean but this complete self-possession in the presence of the peaceful One? There is another of Christ's songs that I would like to repeat unceasingly: "I shall keep my strength for you." (LR 3)

Perhaps Mother Germaine had asked her in these notes to use her own words more, rather than borrowing from others, for she quotes very little from her favorite authors, but the Scriptures had become so very much part of the very fiber of her thought that it was impossible for her not to draw heavily from them.

The notebook she had written for Guite had a certain detachment about it, written in more general terms. The "Last Retreat," though, is more of a spiritual autobiography. Much is written in the first person, and it is almost as if we are overhearing Elizabeth meditating on her own calling, above all her calling as "Praise of Glory." So often there is the impression that she is no longer quoting from Scripture; rather, she is listening to the voice of her "Three" deep within her being; they are teaching her how to become a praise of glory, and the words they speak are the words of Scripture, spoken personally to her, fulfilled and shining out in her.

In several of her letters, Elizabeth said that there was only one preoccupation between herself and the Master now, and that was her preparation for eternity. All else fades away; now she begins her retreat with the one word from the Song of Songs, "Nescivi" (I knew not), and immediately links it with St. Paul's "'Nescivi.'! I no longer know anything, I do not want to know anything except 'to know *Him*, to share in His sufferings, to become like Him in His death'" (LR 1). This referred to the death that was inevitable for her, but more radically it was the death within her of all that was not God. It was the word that enabled her to penetrate the fathomless deeps of God's mystery; to understand and live out more fully the work of praise of glory that will be hers for eternity, but which she must start here and now, in the time which is eternity begun and ever in progress.

"I knew not." This word enabled her to pass continually beyond the distractions, the noise of self, the opinion or opposition of others, seeking the "one thing necessary." Mother Germaine was impressed by how little Elizabeth dwelt on the discomforts and concerns of her illness. While being perfectly open about her pain, she rose above all that it involved with the deceptive simplicity of long practice and the self-forgetfulness that was by now habitual to her. Everything was drawn into that deep inner silence in which she listened not to herself but to what the Master wanted of her, and this gave her an invincible inner strength and self-possession:

> My Rule tells me: "In silence will your strength be." It seems to me, therefore, that to keep one's strength for the Lord is to unify one's whole being by means of interior silence, to collect all one's powers in order to "employ" them in "the one work of love," to have this "single eye" which allows the light of God to enlighten us. A soul that debates with its self, that is taken up with its feelings, and pursues useless thoughts and desires, scatters its forces, for it is not wholly directed toward God. Its lyre does not vibrate in unison and when the Master plays it, He cannot draw from it divine harmonies, for it is still too human and discordant....
>
> How indispensable this beautiful inner unity is for the soul that wants to live here below the life of the blessed....

> It seems to me the Master had that in mind when He
> spoke to Mary Magdalene of the "Unum necessarium."
> (LR 3–4)

Set free by the simplicity of going continually and persistently beyond herself to listen to God's presence within her, Elizabeth was able to fulfill her dream, her calling to be a praise of glory. Praise and adoration—unhindered by self—was her ideal, and love was the power that enabled her to adore even the hand that was crucifying her:

> Adoration, ah! That is a word from Heaven! It seems to
> me it can be defined as the ecstasy of love. It is love over-
> come by the beauty, the strength, the immense grandeur
> of the Object loved, and it "falls down in a kind of faint"
> in an utterly profound silence, that silence of which David
> spoke when he exclaimed: "Silence is Your praise!" Yes,
> this is the most beautiful praise since it is sung eternally
> in the bosom of the tranquil Trinity; and it is also the "last
> effort of the soul that overflows and can say no more..."
> (Lacordaire). (LR 21)

In baptism we are made priests, prophets, and kings, sharing in Christ's own royal, priestly and prophetic character. Her total gift of self gave Elizabeth a truly royal dignity and in describing Christ's bearing, she unconsciously painted a self-portrait in her "Last Retreat":

> "The queen stood at your right hand": such is the attitude
> of this soul; she walks the way of Calvary at the right of
> her crucified, annihilated, humiliated King, yet always so
> strong, so calm, so full of majesty as He goes to His pas-
> sion "to make the glory of His grace blaze forth" accord-
> ing to that so strong expression of St. Paul. He wants to
> associate His Bride in His work of redemption and this
> sorrowful way which she follows seems like the path of
> Beatitude to her, not only because it leads there but also
> because her holy Master makes her realize that she must
> go beyond the bitterness in suffering to find in it, as He
> did, her rest. (LR 13)

All who came into contact with her were profoundly struck by the dignity of her bearing, even when she was racked with pain. A sister came across her in the corridor one day and needed to ask her advice about some matter. Elizabeth answered her with her usual sweetness and calm, and the sister only found out afterward that she was on her way to the tribune to seek strength in prayer after an almost unbearable attack.

Her dignity and self-possession sprang directly from her awareness that she was sharing in her Master's passion through the circumstances of her illness. She was crushed and almost overwhelmed by them, but at the same time she was already being transfigured with the triumph of the resurrection that flowed from her risen Lord's victory, and which would be hers fully on the other side of death.

She was also a prophet. Christian prophecy is not primarily a foretelling of the future, but rather a revealing of God's will and God's purpose in the events of life. It could be said that the whole of Elizabeth's life was prophetic, for so profound was her experience of God that it was almost habitual with her to penetrate beyond external things and events to the presence of the living God within.

The beauty around her always spoke to her of God; she looked at the events of her life and saw God in them—and now above all, in her last illness, to her the reality was not that she was dying of an incurable disease, but that she was being given a share in Christ's cross. She embraced and accepted her illness, not because she sought suffering for its own sake, but because by it and through it she was becoming more like her adored Master, and therefore she felt no bitterness or resentment.

She was both priest and victim as Jesus was. Night was perhaps the most difficult time for her, and she told Mother Marie of Jesus during a visit that when she went to bed, it was as if she were climbing onto her altar. When her pain became almost too much to bear, she would kiss her crucifix and gently calm herself down and tell him, "My God, that does not count" (LR 2).

If her infirmary bed was her altar, she saw Mother Germaine as the priest offering her to God. But she, too, was priest, offering the sacrifice of herself, offering him the constant sacrifice of praise that was his due, praise that was truly sacrificial precisely because it rose up from the heart of her pain. She longed to be a spotless sacrifice with a holiness that was not of her own making but was Christ's own. Like Jesus, she emptied herself continually so that he would fill her. With Jesus, she offered herself for souls, coredemptrix sharing in his work of salvation.

She ended her "Last Retreat" on a similar note of triumph as in "Heaven in Faith," which was also a self-portrait:

> How beautiful is this creature thus stripped, freed from self! It can "use the ascensions in its heart so that it may pass from this valley of tears" (that is, from all that is less than God) "to the place which is its goal," this "Spacious place" of which the psalmist sings, which is, it seems to me, the unfathomable Trinity "Immensus Pater, immensus Filius, immensus Spiritus sanctus!" It ascends, it rises above the senses, above nature; it transcends itself; it goes beyond every joy and every pain and passes through the clouds, not stopping until it has penetrated "*into the interior*" of Him whom it loves and who Himself will give it "the repose of the abyss." And all that without leaving the holy fortress! The Master had said to it: "Hurry and *come down*...." It is also without leaving it that the soul will live, like the immutable Trinity, in an *eternal present*, "adoring Him always because of Himself," and becoming by an always more simple, more unitive gaze, "the splendor of His glory," that is, the unceasing praise of glory of His adorable perfections. (LR 44)

15

THE GREATNESS OF OUR VOCATION

By the end of August, Elizabeth had become so weak and emaciated that she was no longer able to receive visits from her friends. Her voice was so feeble that the concentration and the effort needed to make herself heard behind the closed shutters of the parlor grilles was too much for her. Her family, though, was able to see her in the small infirmary parlor with the shutters open, which was less of a strain.

As the summer days drew to an end and with it the warm weather, her mother was worried about the cold that would soon penetrate Carmel's cloisters. Elizabeth hastened to reassure her; she had a small stove in her infirmary cell that the sisters were already urging her to use but which she had asked not to be lit yet; "I'll no longer be able to leave the fireside once I'm settled there, and then adieu, my dear little tribune I love so much!" (L 314).

She did ask her mother, though, to send her a Pyrenean cape she had had before entering if they still had it, and Mme. Catez brought with her in the middle of September a large cloak as well. She also sent some samples of material that she thought could be made into a warm robe. Elizabeth was touched by her mother's thoughtfulness, but it also put her in a bit of a quandary. "It concerns me there is no question of holy poverty but only of charity" (L 314), she wrote back. She explained that Mother Germaine had already asked the robier to measure her for a new habit, warm and much lighter than the normal Carmelite habit, which was now too heavy for her. Elizabeth therefore suggested her mother's material could be made into an underskirt.

Her family also continued to keep her supplied with chocolate and cheese and whatever else she could manage to eat. Guite gave her some Klauss chocolate that she found easier to digest than the Suchard chocolate Mother Germaine bought for her. Such things were no longer luxuries for her but were managing to keep her alive.

Mother Germaine, too, could not do enough for her. Elizabeth wrote:

> This good Mother, who is so inspiring about the ways of immolation, thinks of nothing but giving me comfort, which I often point out to her, but I let myself become like a little child, and the Master told our holy Mother Teresa. He preferred her obedience to the penance of another saint. So I accept the little favors, like the candy and chocolates when my stomach allows it, and that's what makes it suffer the least these days. Many thanks to Georges for the case of milk. I am deeply grateful to him for his kindness to his little sister; I like very much to have my soup with this milk, which doesn't curdle like the other, but I admit that digesting it is also painful: a single spoonful really hurts me, and if I try to force myself, it causes an attack.... You can see I'm attentive to my stomach and, for love of God, I do what I can to not let it die of hunger. (L 309)

She was still able to walk, and since the nights were so difficult for her, she usually tried to stay up to follow the night office from the tribune, where she could also follow the Divine Office during the day. Her indomitable spirit drove her on. One evening, suffering even more than usual and feeling totally exhausted, she was tempted to go to bed but forced herself to stay up. When Mother Germaine said afterward she should have gone to bed and united her prayer with the community's from there, she replied, "I thought that would be cowardly, Mother, so I got up from my armchair and knelt down to pray with even greater faith because of my lack of courage. My Master gave me so much strength that now I find it much easier to wait until after compline before I go to bed" (Souv. 222). Far from praying for an ease to her suffering, she prayed only for a greater capacity to bear the pain.

On September 9 she wrote what was to be her last letter to her friend Françoise, "Framboise" de Sourdon, who was now nineteen.

Over the years she had patiently and lovingly guided the often willful and temperamental young girl, becoming like a spiritual mother to her. Realizing that Elizabeth did not have much longer to live, Framboise apparently wrote to her, asking her advice on various matters. Elizabeth took this opportunity to write what she jokingly called her "treatise," a spiritual testament that would be her last gift to the young woman she loved so tenderly.

It took her several days to write; her physical weakness was now so great that she had to write with a pencil rather than a pen. But her mind had lost none of its clarity of thought, and reading the treatise's four tightly written pages with its precise development and its serene spaciousness, it is difficult to realize that she was often almost fainting with pain as she wrote it.

In many ways she saw herself in the high-spirited and idealistic younger woman, who needed guidance for her idealism to be directed and tempered. In her "treatise" she could fire Framboise with her own vast vision and at the same time nourish her with the very sane, practical, and down-to-earth advice which was the bedrock on which her own life of intense union with God was grounded:

> Here comes Sabeth at last to sit down by her dearest Framboise and visit—with her *pencil*! I say pencil for the heart-to-heart communion was established long ago, and we are now as one. How I love our evening rendez-vous; it is like the prelude of that communion from Heaven to earth that will be established between our souls. It seems to me that I am like a mother bending attentively over her favorite child: I raise my eyes and look at God, and then I lower them on you, exposing you to the rays of His Love. Framboise, I do not use words when I speak to Him of you but He understands me even better for He prefers my silence. My dearest child, I wish I were a saint so that I could help you here below while waiting to do it from Heaven. What I would not endure in order to obtain for you the graces of strength that you need.
>
> I want to answer your questions. Let's treat humility first; I have read some splendid pages on it in the book I spoke to you about. The pious author says that nothing can

"disturb" the humble. He possesses "invincible peace for he has plunged into such an abyss that no one would go that far to look for him." He also says that the humble person finds his greatest pleasure in life in feeling his own "weakness" "before God." Little Framboise, pride is not something that is destroyed with one good blow of the sword! Doubtless, certain heroic acts of humility, such as we read of in the lives of the saints, give it, if not a mortal blow, at least one that considerably weakens it; but without that grace we must put it to death each day! "Quotidie morior," exclaimed St. Paul, "I die daily!"

...this doctrine of dying to self is the law for every Christian, for Christ said: "If anyone wants to follow Me, let him take up his cross and deny himself." But this doctrine which seems so austere, takes on a delightful sweetness when we consider the outcome of this death—life in God in place of our life of sin and misery. That is what St. Paul meant when he wrote: "Strip off the old man and clothe yourselves anew in the image of Him who created you." This image is God Himself. Do you recall His wish which He so clearly expressed on the day of creation: "Let us make man in our image and likeness"? Oh! you see, if we would think more about the origin of our soul, things here below would seem so childish that we would have only contempt for them. St. Peter writes in one of his epistles that "we have been made sharers in His divine nature." And St. Paul recommends that we "hold firm to the end this beginning of His existence which He has given us."

It seems to me the soul that is aware of its greatness enters into that "holy freedom of the children of God" of which the Apostle speaks, that is, it transcends all things, including self. The freest soul, I think, is the one most forgetful of self. If anyone were to ask me the secret of happiness, I would say it is to no longer think of self, to deny oneself always. That is a good way to kill pride: let it starve to death! You see, pride is love of ourselves; well, love of God must be so strong that it extinguishes all our self-love. St. Augustine says we have two cities within us, the city of God and the city of SELF. To the extent that the first increases, the second will be destroyed. A soul that lives by faith in God's presence, that has this "single eye" that Christ speaks of in the Gospel, that is, a purity of "intention" that seeks only God; this soul, it seems to me, would also live in humility: it would recognize His gifts to it—for "humility is truth"—but it would attribute nothing to itself, referring all to God as the Blessed Virgin did.

...all the movements of pride that you feel within yourself, only become faults when the will takes part in them! Without that, although you may suffer much, you are not offending God. Doubtless self-love is at the bottom of those faults which, as you say, you commit without thinking, but that, my poor darling, is, in a way, part of us.... What God asks of you is never to entertain deliberately any thought of pride, and never to act on the inspiration of pride, for this is wrong. And yet, if you find yourself doing either of these, you must not become discouraged, for again, it is pride which is irritated. You must "display your misery" like Magdalene at the Master's feet, and ask Him to set you free. He so loves to see a soul recognize its weakness. Then, as a great saint said, "The abyss of God's immensity encounters the abyss of the creature's nothingness," and God embraces this nothingness.

My dearest child, it is not pride to think that you do not want to live an easy life; I truly believe that God wants your life to be spent in a realm where the air breathed is divine. Oh! You see, I have a profound compassion for souls that live only for this world and its trivialities; I consider them as slaves, and I wish I could tell them: Shake off the yoke that weighs you down; what are you doing with these bonds that chain you to yourself and to things less than yourself? It seems to me that the happy ones of this world are those who have enough contempt and forgetfulness of self to choose the Cross as their lot! What delightful peace we experience when we place our joy in suffering!

"In my own flesh I fill up what is lacking in the passion of Christ for the sake of His body, which is the Church." The apostle finds his happiness in this! The thought pursues me and I confess that I experience a profound inner joy in thinking that God has chosen to associate me in the passion of His Christ. This way of Calvary I climb each day seems to me more like the path of Beatitude! Have you ever seen those pictures depicting death reaping with his sickle? Well, that is my condition; I seem to feel myself being destroyed like that. Sometimes it is painful for nature and I can assure you that if I were to remain at that level, I would feel only my cowardice in the face of suffering. But that is looking at things from the human point of view! Very quickly "I open the eye of my soul in the light of faith." And this faith tells me that it is love who is destroying me, who is slowly consuming me; then I feel a tremendous joy, and I surrender myself to Him as His prey.

...to attain the ideal life of the soul, I believe we must live on the supernatural level, that is, we must never act "naturally." We must become aware that God dwells within us and do everything with Him, then we are never commonplace, even when performing the most ordinary tasks, for we do not live in these things, we go beyond them! A supernatural soul never deals with secondary causes but with God alone. Oh! How its life is simplified, how it resembles the life of the blessed, how it is freed from self and from all things! Everything for it is reduced to unity, to that "one thing necessary," of which the Master spoke to Magdalene. Then the soul is truly great, truly free, for it has "*enclosed its will in God's.*"

...when we contemplate our eternal predestination, visible things seem so worthless. Listen to St. Paul: "Those whom God has foreknown, He has also predestined to be conformed to the image of His Son." (That is not all, my little one, you are going to see that you are one of the number of the "known"!) "And those He has known He has called": it is baptism which has made you a child of adoption, which has stamped you with a seal of the Holy Trinity! "And those whom He has called, He has also justified": how often you have been justified by the sacrament of penance and by all those touches of God in your soul, without you even being aware of it!

"And those whom He justified, He has also glorified." That is what awaits you in eternity! But remember that our degree of glory will depend on the degree of grace in which God finds us at the moment of death; allow him to complete His work of predestination in you. To do this listen to St. Paul again who will give you a program of life.

"Walk in Jesus Christ, rooted in Him, built up on Him, strengthened in faith and growing in Him in thanksgiving." Yes, little child of my heart and soul, walk in Jesus Christ: you need this broad road, for you were not made for the narrow paths of here below! Be *rooted* in Him. This implies being uprooted from self, or doing everything as if you were, by denying self each time you meet it. *Be built* up on Him, high above everything that is passing, there where everything is pure, everything is luminous.

Be *strengthened in faith*, that is, never act except in the great light of God, never according to impressions of your imagination. Believe that He loves you, that He wants to help you in the struggles you have to undergo. Believe in His love, His *exceeding* love, as St. Paul says. Nourish your soul on the great thoughts of faith which will reveal to you all its richness and the end for which God has created you! If you live like this, your piety will never be a nervous exaltation as you fear but will be *true*. Truth is so beautiful, the truth of love. "He loved me and gave Himself up for me." That, my little child, is what it means to be true!

And, finally, *grow in thanksgiving*. That is the last word of the program and is but the consequence of it. If you walk rooted in Christ, strengthened in your faith, you will live in thanksgiving: the love of the sons of God! I wonder how a soul that has sounded the depths of love the Heart of God has "*for it*" could be anything but joyful in every suffering and sorrow. Remember that "He has chosen you in Him before the creation of the world to be immaculate and pure in His presence in love"; again it is St. Paul who says this. So do not fear struggles or temptations: "When I am weak," exclaimed the Apostle, "it is then I am strong, for the strength of Jesus Christ dwells in me."

I wonder what our Reverend Mother is going to think when she sees this journal. She does not let me write any more for I am extremely weak, and I feel as if I would faint at any moment. This will probably be the last letter from your Sabeth; it has taken her many days to write, and that explains its incoherence. And yet this evening I cannot bring myself to leave you. I am in solitude; it is seven-thirty, and the community is at recreation. As for me, I feel already as if I were almost in heaven here in my little cell, alone with Him alone, bearing my cross with my Master. Framboise, my happiness increases along with my suffering! If you only knew how delicious the dregs are at the bottom of the chalice prepared by my Heavenly Father! (GV 1–13)

Mme. Catez spent September with Guite and her family, looking after the children for her and making the underskirt for Elizabeth. On her return to Dijon at the beginning of October, she came to see her daughter every day, distressed at the deterioration she could see in her. But Elizabeth was well enough to join in various community celebrations during the month. She was able to join them in choir for the first time in seven months for the celebration of St. Teresa's death at the beginning of the month, and that same afternoon in a simple ceremony she received the new habit that had been made for her. Just as at her clothing ceremony, it was blessed, and Elizabeth followed every detail of the ceremonial, even observing the great prostration by which she renewed the commitment she had made at her first clothing ceremony.

On the three days leading up to St. Teresa's feast day, October 15, they celebrated the Carmelite martyrs of Compiègne, whose beatifications were announced that day. Guite and Georges, who was also an excellent musician, arranged the music for the ceremony, and Elizabeth helped as much as she could with arranging the flowers. Abbé Vallée gave talks for the three days and during this time saw Elizabeth for the last time in the parlor. She spoke to him of her desire for suffering, but he told her not to limit herself to that. It was God she longed for, it was he she should yield to, leaving him free to act in any way he chose. "Elizabeth's last days," Abbé Vallée later wrote to Mme Catez, were "so uncommonly, so divinely beautiful" (PG xi). Then on the feast day itself the bishop of Dijon, Msgr. Dadolle, announced the beatifications of the new martyrs and preached the sermon.

Then the following week there was the clothing ceremony for a young lay sister, Marie Joseph of Our Lady of Grace, with Guite and Georges again helping out with the music. Knowing the joy it would give her fellow-novice if she were involved in some way, Elizabeth insisted on sewing the white veil she would be given that day. By this time her body was almost reduced to a skeleton, and she needed all her mental energy to make the smallest movement. Her fingers could hardly hem the linen and often fell helplessly on her table, but she would allow no one to take over the task. This was one last little act of love she could do for her sister.

Mme. Catez attended the clothing ceremony on October 22. In the parlor afterward she could see that Elizabeth's mouth and tongue were on fire due to a severe inner inflammation, making talking excruciating for her, yet immense joy simply radiated from her face. Friends who were with her left in tears.

A priest who gave her Holy Communion found it a harrowing experience.

> I'll never forget the impression your angelic daughter made on me when I gave her Holy Communion three weeks before she died," he wrote to Mme. Catez later. "I had been warned, but when I saw her tongue red as if on fire I was so unnerved that my hand was trembling as I laid the sacred host on it. I considered it one of the greatest graces of my priestly ministry given me by the Sacred Heart that I was able to bring her the consolation of Holy Communion when she was so soon to be crowned in heaven. Our Lord seemed to want me to understand that the love which burned in his holy victim was far more fiery than the fire that was consuming her body. (Souv. 247–248)

But the suffering was becoming almost too much for her to bear, even for someone as courageous as Elizabeth. That evening she wrote a short note to her prioress:

> My beloved priest, Your little victim is suffering very, very much, it is a kind of physical agony. She feels so cowardly, cowardly enough to scream! But the Being who is the Fullness of Love visits her, keeps her company, makes her enter into communion with Him, while He makes her understand that as long as He leaves her on earth, He will measure out suffering to her. (L 329)

One day Mother Germaine came to see her; as they talked together Elizabeth showed the same serenity as she always did, but just as the prioress was leaving, she indicated the window and remarked,

"Mother, are you happy leaving me alone like this?" Mother Germaine didn't know what to make of the remark, and Elizabeth continued, "I'm suffering so much that I understand now how people can commit suicide. But don't worry, God is looking after me."

"And yet," Mother Germaine remarked, "she had witnessed in our conversation together, as always, how happy she was to suffer." This was the paradox, the divine paradox, at the heart of Elizabeth's last weeks, and in this, too, she was like her Master. Jesus had longed for his passion and yet pleaded with his Father in the garden of Gethsemane to take the cup from him. The pain could make Elizabeth almost suicidal, yet she could be radiantly joyful that she was thus suffering.

The secret lay in a remark she had made to her mother, writing to her at the end of September: "I cannot say I love suffering in itself, but I love it because it conforms me to Him who is my Bridegroom and my Love. Oh, you see, that bestows such sweet peace, such profound joy on the soul, and you end up putting your happiness in everything that is irritating" (L 317).

This was a true and genuine peace. At the same time as she was writing to her mother, she was composing some verses for the anniversary of Mother Germaine's profession on September 24, and they beautifully expressed this tranquillity and peace that lay deep within her:

> Peaceful was the night and deep the silence
> When my boat set sail on the open sea,
> Gliding over the boundless ocean on the loveliest of
>   journeys.
> All was hushed beneath the vault of heaven
> As if listening to the voice of the Eternal.
> Suddenly the waves arose,
> engulfing my light barque—
> It was the Trinity opening out to me:
> In that divine abyss I found my deepest center.
> No more will you find me at the water's edge;
> I have plunged into infinity, where I belong.
> With my Three I live at peace,
> In the wide freedom of eternity." (P 11)

As she had explained in her letter to Framboise, if she had listened to human nature, she would have given in long ago. But because she continually fixed her eyes on "the wide freedom of eternity," the infinity of her "Three," which was her home where she belonged, she could embrace her appalling sufferings with incredible courage and self-control.

She had now dubbed her infirmary cell "The Palace of Pain and Bliss," a telling phrase that captured the paradox, and wrote to Mother Germaine from that "palace" early in October:

> Your little praise of glory cannot sleep, she is suffering; but in her soul, although the anguish penetrates there too, she feels so much peace, and it is your visit that has brought this Heavenly peace. Her little heart needs to tell you this, and in her tender gratitude she is praying and suffering unceasingly for you! Oh, help me climb my Calvary; I feel the power of your priesthood over my soul so strongly, and I need you so much. My Mother, I feel my Three so close to me; I am more overwhelmed by happiness than by pain: my Master has reminded me that it is my dwelling place and I am not to choose my sufferings; so I immerse myself with Him into immense suffering, with much fear and anguish. (L 320)

Elizabeth had been in Carmel just over five years. Before her entry then, she had written her last letters to friends and relatives before Carmel's doors closed behind her. Now, with death coming ever closer, as she lived through her '"novitiate for heaven" with the last remnants of strength she still possessed, she now wrote final letters once more to her wide circle of friends. Many of them she thanked for gifts of chocolate, small tokens of their love and concern that they showered upon her once they knew that was all she could manage to eat. She wrote to her old friend Anne-Marie Maurel, now Anne-Marie d'Avout; to Clémence Blanc, the young girl who had left Carmel a few months earlier; and to Marthe Weishardt, another ex-novice. To Mme. de Bobet, a family friend, she wrote a long letter that almost read like a last will and testament, echoing Jesus' own words to his disciples the night before he died:

The hour is drawing near when I am going to pass from this world to my Father, and before leaving I want to send you a note from my heart, a testament from my soul. Never was the Heart of the Master so overflowing with love as at the supreme moment when He was going to leave His own! It seems to me as if something similar is happening in His little bride at the evening of her life, and I feel as if a wave were rising from my heart to yours! ...in the light of eternity the soul sees things as they really are. Oh! how empty is all that has not been done for God and with God! I beg you, oh, mark everything with the seal of love! It alone endures. How serious life is: each minute is given us in order to "root" us deeper in God, as Saint Paul says, so the resemblance to our divine Model may be more striking, the union more intimate. But to accomplish this plan, which is that of God Himself, here is the secret: forget self, give up self, ignore self, look at the Master, look only at Him, accept as coming directly from His love both joy and suffering; this places the soul on such serene heights!...

...I leave you my faith in the presence of God, of the God who is all Love dwelling in our souls. I confide to you: it is this intimacy with Him "within" that has been the beautiful sun illuminating my life, making it already an anticipated Heaven; it is what sustains me today in my suffering. I do not fear my weakness; that's what gives me confidence. For the Strong One is within me and His power is almighty. It is able to do, says the Apostle, abundantly more than we can hope for! A Dieu, my Antoinette, when I am up above, will you let me help you, scold you even, if I see you are not giving everything to the Master? because I love you! (L 333)

16

PRAISE OF GLORY

"I think the last 'veni' will not be long in coming; she is really going downhill, the little saint," Mother Germaine wrote to Mme. de Sourdon, October 9. "Another month, six weeks perhaps..." (L 323, n. 7).

She was to prove remarkably accurate. When her family came to see Elizabeth on October 29, though, her mother thought she was a tiny bit stronger; she was able to speak a little better, and she thought they might well be able to see her one more time. Elizabeth's two nieces, Sabeth and Odile, were there, and Guite made them kneel at the grille so that Elizabeth, lovingly and with a touching dignity, could bless them with her large profession crucifix.

She was able to spend some time with them, but as they were saying good-bye, Elizabeth said quietly to her mother, "Mother, when the turn sister comes to tell you that my sufferings are over, kneel down and say, 'My God, you gave her to me, I give her back to you; your holy name be blessed!'" (Souv. 251).

It proved to be the last time they saw her, and also the last time she was to leave her infirmary cell. The following day she was too ill to leave her cell to visit the tribune she loved so much, although when Mother Germaine visited her during the day, she was pale but happy. Gazing at a picture of Teresa of Avila on the wall of her cell, she reflected that Teresa's glory in heaven was due more to the depth of her love than to all the great deeds she had done. "And we have loved each other so much," she added, pressing her profession crucifix to her heart. "At the evening of my life this is what matters most to me.... All I want now is to live by love" (Souv. 251–252).

Only a short while before, she had experienced an invasion of that love. One morning Mother Germaine came in to see her, and Elizabeth exclaimed:

> Mother, a little more and you wouldn't have found
> Laudem Gloriae on earth any more! Yesterday evening I
> felt as if I was suffering a complete inner collapse, when
> all of a sudden I felt as if I was being invaded by Love.
> It's impossible to describe what I experienced; it was a fire
> of infinite sweetness and at the same time I felt it wound-
> ing me mortally. I believe if it had lasted much longer I
> would have died. (Souv. 248)

It was a gift of love that would carry her through the final days of her Calvary.

The day after her family's visit, she wouldn't stay in bed, saying she was so exhausted that if she did, she might never be able to leave it again. She finally went to bed just before matins, and when Mother Germaine came in to see her after the Divine Office, she found her recovering from a fit of shivering that had shaken the whole bed. Elizabeth was overjoyed to see her, afraid that she might have died before her prioress arrived. By now, at last, she was being given sleeping medicine to give her some relief at night, and she eventually drifted off to sleep until three o'clock when the intense pain woke her once more.

Hearing a slight noise, Mother Germaine went in to her, and the two of them spent an unforgettable hour together, Elizabeth's joy at the prospect of soon seeing her beloved Master transcending her pain. During the day she received the last sacraments again, and as the bells began to ring, heralding the eve of All Saints, Elizabeth was convinced they were ringing, too, for her own entry into heaven.

"Those bells are making me die with joy!" she exclaimed, "Oh, let me go!" By ten o'clock the next morning the community did indeed think her time had come, and they assembled in the infirmary to say the prayers for the dying with her.

It was not to be, just yet, though; she recovered from her collapse and, perhaps because her hopes were dashed after the intensity of her joy the previous day, she entered into a sort of inner darkness, which made her almost unendurable sufferings even worse. But she accepted this with her usual courage; just as Jesus' physical agony on the cross was compounded by his sense of abandonment by his Father, so

Elizabeth had to drain the cup of a similar sense of abandonment and inner agony.

"It would have been too easy to die in the state of soul I was in then," she remarked. "I'll go in pure faith and I like that much better; I'll be even more like my Master and it will be more real (Souv. 255). "I feel as if my body is suspended and that my soul is in darkness," she said of the next few days. "But I know it is Love's doing, and I'm glad" (Souv. 255).

A sister asked her to describe her pain. For a few seconds Elizabeth's face collapsed in a grimace as if, she had expressed at times, wild beasts were tearing her entrails out, and then her face returned to its normal serenity of expression. From now on she could swallow nothing, not even the few barley sugar drops that had been her last source of nourishment. She took a few drops of water only at the cost of severe pain and was suffering torments of thirst—just as her Master had done on the cross, she noted joyfully.

Elizabeth received Holy Communion for the last time on the feast of All Saints, for after that she was unable to swallow even the smallest particle of the host. "I find him now on the cross," she said. "It is from there he gives me life" (Souv. 256).

With her mouth dried up and parched, she suffered acute cerebral pain; the threat of meningitis was only averted by the constant application of ice, which melted on contact due to the intense inner heat she was enduring. She felt as if her brain was on fire, her eyes were bloodshot, and she could hardly open her eyes at all. It was incredible under the circumstances, then, that she was still able to think of others at this time. No longer able to write, she dictated letters instead, one of them to her doctor, thanking him for his care of her: "My heart is borrowing the hand of my Mother to tell you again one last time how grateful it is to you for the good care you have lavished on me during these months of sufferings that have been months of blessings, profound joys unknown by the world" (L 340).

After her own family, those closest to her had been the Hallos, and the last two letters she dictated to Mother Germaine were for them. One was written to Mme. Hallo, her "second mother," the last one of all was to Charles Hallo, her childhood friend and her staunch companion as they grew up together. Following in his father's footsteps, he was now in the army, and it was as from one soldier, whose valiant fight was almost done, to another that she wrote:

> Before going to Heaven your Elizabeth wants to tell you once more of her deep affection for you and her plan to help you, day by day, until you join her in Heaven. My darling Charles, I want you to walk in the footsteps of your father, in the valiant faith that keeps the will always faithful. You will have battles to fight, my little brother, you will encounter obstacles on the path of life, but do not be discouraged, call me. Yes, call your little sister; in this way you will increase her happiness in Heaven; she will be so glad to help you triumph, to remain worthy of God, of your venerable father, of your mother, whose joy you must be. I no longer have the strength to dictate these last wishes of a very loving sister. When I am close to God, recollect yourself in prayer and we will meet each other in an even deeper way. I am leaving you a medal from my rosary; wear it always in memory of your Elizabeth who will love you even more in Heaven! (L 342)

The same tender thoughtfulness marked her love for her sisters in Carmel, too. When Sr. Marie-Xavier, the sacristan, heard Elizabeth being called by her "new name," Laudem Gloriae, she wanted a "new name" for herself, too. On the eve of All Saints, Elizabeth had a little scrap of paper put in her cell with the words "Abscondita in Deo"—Hidden in God, another quotation from St. Paul—written on it. Marie-Xavier was intrigued and longed to speak to Elizabeth about it, so that she could explain it more deeply to her. When Elizabeth became so gravely ill that day, though, she thought she would never have the opportunity to do so. She was amazed, therefore, when on November 5, when she was sitting alone by Elizabeth's bedside, Elizabeth clasped her hand and, peering through her bloodshot, half-open eyes, said in a barely audible voice,

"You're 'Abscondita', aren't you?"

"Yes."

"Well, he gave you that name himself, I understood it. What a program! 'Abscondita in Deo' means separation from earthly things, it is a continual turning to him. What self-denial, prayer, self-forgetfulness that name demands! I can't tell you all, but I'll be helping you from heaven" (Souv. 258–259).

Her sisters were struck by the fact that, even threatened by meningitis and with a high fever that would normally make a patient delirious, Elizabeth still had her thoughts under control. Her union with God was so complete and habitual that not even in those circumstances did her thoughts or her orientation toward him falter. "In appearance all but dead, she lived in God," Mother Germaine remarked (Souv. 257), which was all that Elizabeth wanted. "I am 'Elizabeth of the Trinity,'" she had once written to Germaine de Gemeaux, "that is, Elizabeth disappearing, losing herself, letting herself be invaded by the Three" (L 172). It could be said that she no longer prayed; as one sister remarked, she had become prayer.

She longed above all to be transfigured into Christ Crucified, and even her body shared in this likeness. Sometimes her face was as sorrowful as that of her Master, the Man of Sorrows, was in his Passion; sometimes she looked like a young child; sometimes she had the dignity of a queen.

"I'll never forget the impression she made on me those last nine days," said the subprioress, Marie of the Trinity. "On the one hand it was deeply moving to see her poor body, totally unrecognizable, which made one think of Jesus being taken down from the Cross; and on the other hand, I had a profound admiration for her, so utterly was she taken up into the great mystery of the world to come that it was impossible for her to describe what was happening to her" (Souv. 259).

This thought of heaven, though, which had always made her life a heaven on earth, began during the early days of November to reveal its awesome and even fearful side to her. She was able to enter into the experience of those to whom the thought of death and God's judgment brought only fear and apprehension. She, who in knowing God, knew heaven, found herself confronted by the awesome unknowingness of it, too.

"The thought of heaven thrills me," she said.

> I seem to have lived there for so long, but it is unknown.... I wouldn't mind spending eternity praying for the dying, helping them. There is something terrifying about death! ...It must be dreadful for those who have spent their days interested only in worldly pleasures. Even though I am free of that, I still feel an undefinable sense of the justice and the holiness of God. I know death is a punishment and I'm so poor, of so little worth. (Souv. 260)

One evening, Sr. Agnes of Jesus, seeing her in agony, said, "My poor little sister, you can't bear any more, can you?"

"No, I can't bear any more."

"You long for heaven, don't you?"

"Yes. Until now I have surrendered myself to him, but I'm his bride and I have the right to say to him, 'Let us go!' We love each other so much, I'm longing to see him. Oh, I love him so much!" (Souv. 262).

The Lord willed that meeting to be a few more days, though, willed that she spend herself a little longer drop by drop for his glory and for the church, as she herself expressed it. The expression on her face began to change as her inner darkness began to give way to light. Her final days seemed to fix her beyond suffering and, like her beloved St. Paul, she was given glimpses of the heaven that would soon be hers in all its fullness, experiences that defied description.

One night she dreamed of a beautiful palace of white and gold, and inside the palace was a bride, very tall but of such lovely proportions that she was of incomparable majesty. "Perhaps it was Laudem Gloriae," suggested one of the sisters.

"I don't know," replied Elizabeth, smiling. "I didn't see her face, but she was so beautiful! So beautiful! The dream has given me such heavenly joy" (Souv. 262).

Another morning she was seen to peer through half-shut eyes, leaning forward slightly as if looking at something. "What are you doing?" asked the sister with her.

"I can see a palm," and she made a gesture as if taking hold of something.

"A palm?"

"Yes, a beautiful palm."

"Is it for you?"

"I don't know; but I'm not selfish, I would like all my sisters to have one, too" (Souv. 262).

A little later she gave a small exclamation and gesture to show that she saw herself surrounded by a radiance: "It is full of light! It's wonderful! ...It's..." (Souv. 262) but the words failed her.

The day before she died, the doctor, to her intense joy, told her that her pulse was so weak that she could only have a day or two at the most to live. "In two days I shall probably be with my Three. Isn't that wonderful! I was glad when they said to me.... It will be Mary, full of light, so pure with the purity of God himself, who will take me by the hand and lead me into heaven, that heaven so full of dazzling light" (Souv. 263).

She couldn't hide her delight from the doctor, who couldn't understand the depth of her faith and her happiness. She tried to put it into words, tried to explain the ineffable, but that last effort totally exhausted her. She was too weak after that to speak; she was plunged into the silence she loved so much, and which alone would express far more than words. Only from time to time did the sisters hear her say in a kind of chant, "I am going to Light, to Life, to Love!" These were the last words she spoke.

They summed up her life. From the silence of her heart, from the silence of her life from which all self-love had been silenced, was distilled the pure essence of which her life had been composed: light, life, love.

The night of November 8 to 9 was extremely painful; a sense of suffocation was now added to the other tortures that racked her body.

Toward dawn, though, her sufferings eased a little and she became calmer. As she lay on her bed, now silent and peaceful, her sisters came and knelt round her as the first Angelus bell began to ring. Elizabeth lay on her right side, her head thrown back slightly, her eyes wide-open now, fixed on a point just over their heads, in ecstasy rather than agony. Her face was wonderfully beautiful, and the sisters could not take their eyes off her. It seemed as if she was already looking at heaven.

About 6:15 P.M., still with that radiant expression, she died so peacefully that they couldn't be sure of the exact moment. It was all over.

EPILOGUE: LET YOURSELF BE LOVED

Elizabeth of the Trinity died on November 9, the feast of the Dedication of the Basilica of the Holy Savior. As the sisters recited the liturgy of the day, so many of the words and prayers seemed totally appropriate to Elizabeth herself, who had truly been a house of prayer and a temple of the Holy Spirit: "The Lord has sanctified his tabernacle.... My house will be called a house of prayer.... O Bride! how blessed is your lot!. You are gifted with the glory of the Father, filled with the grace of the Bridegroom, espoused to Christ, your King!" (*Office of the Dedication of a Church*).

One of the extern sisters went round to Mme. Catez's house to break the news to her. She uttered an agonized cry, and the sister gently reminded her of what Elizabeth had said at their last visit. Mme. Catez sank down on her knees and said as her daughter had wished, "The Lord has given, the Lord has taken away; blessed be the name of the Lord."

For the next three days Elizabeth's body lay in choir, surrounded by flowers, the statue of Janua Coeli on a table beside the opened coffin. Her sisters, who had loved her so dearly and whom she had loved so much in turn, kept constant watch by her.

As news of her death spread through Dijon, visitors crowded in the chapel to see her and to pray by her coffin. To many who had known her well, it was a harrowing experience, because her illness had so ravaged her body that they could scarcely recognize her.

Elizabeth's funeral was truly a triumph, her Requiem Mass celebrated by twenty-four priests and with many family, friends, and acquaintances making up the procession. It was a tribute to one who had longed to lose herself, to disappear so that her Lord might be glorified, and who yet had qualities that drew people to her, won over by her radiance, her love, and the beauty of holiness of one who transparently lived so close to God.

Those who followed her coffin to the cemetery were but a foretaste of the many who would be drawn by the example of her life and her prayer in the years to come, a mission she had sensed herself. Two weeks before she died, Elizabeth had written to Sr. Marie Odile, who had been with her in the novitiate at Dijon and who was now at Paray-le-Monial: "I think that in Heaven my mission will be to draw souls by helping them go out of themselves to cling to God by a wholly simple and loving movement, and to keep them in this great silence within that will allow God to communicate Himself to them and transform them into Himself" (L 335). This was what she herself had lived.

With the funeral over, Mother Germaine of Jesus especially must have felt the days very empty without the daughter she had loved so much. During the last months of Elizabeth's illness, she had been almost constantly by her bedside. Often Elizabeth, seeing her exhaustion, had urged her to rest, but with those two women it was a question of mutual love, mutual self-giving.

From Elizabeth's very first days in Carmel, there had been a rare and precious bond between them. Both of them loved Carmel, loved the traditions of the order and the spiritual teachings handed down by the great Carmelite saints: Teresa of Avila, John of the Cross, and Thérèse of Lisieux. The strong and virile love of God that Teresa of Avila had bequeathed to her daughters was theirs in full measure. But Germaine's timidity and diffidence about her abilities made her fearful that she was not living up to the responsibilities required of her in guiding and inspiring the fervent and generous community in her charge.

During the course of Elizabeth's illness, their roles of guide and disciple became reversed in many ways; during Elizabeth's short life in Carmel, Germaine trained her lovingly and surely, opening up her capacity for courageous generosity that would enable her to tread her painful Calvary. Germaine had been the beloved priest offering Elizabeth up on the altar of pain and sacrifice.

As Elizabeth soared with giant steps toward yet greater union with God and transformation in Christ, Germaine knew in her humility that her protégé was far outstripping her on her way to holiness. It was Elizabeth's turn, therefore, to be "priest" to her prioress, discerning, in her timidity and reserve, Mother Germaine's sense of unworthiness, a disbelief, even, that God could really love her, which was perhaps deepened before Elizabeth's own exceptional and heroic example.

It was typical of Elizabeth's unfailing thoughtfulness, therefore, when, after her death, a small white envelope addressed to her prioress was found among her effects, a last message from her beloved daughter. She wanted to inspire Mother Germaine with her own unswerving confidence in God's immense and unfailing love for her, which had been the bedrock of Elizabeth's own life of love. Her total trust that a loving hand was allowing her to suffer gave purpose to her pain and the courage and triumphant will to be like her crucified Lord.

Mother Germaine treasured this last letter so much that, although she sometimes spoke of it, it was only after she herself died in 1934 that it was found in her grace book, much worn by frequent handling, and her sisters were able to read it for themselves:

> My Cherished Mother, my Holy Priest, when you read these lines, your little Praise of Glory will no longer be singing on earth, but will be living in Love's immense furnace; so you can believe her and listen to her as "the voice" of God. Cherished Mother, I would have liked to tell you all that you have been for me, but the hour is so serious, so solemn…and I don't want to delay over telling you things that I think lose something when trying to express them in words. What your child is coming to do is to reveal to you what she feels, or, to be more exact; what her God, in the hours of profound recollection, of unifying contact, makes her understand.
>
> *"You are uncommonly loved,"* loved by that love of preference that the Master had here below for some and which brought them so far. He does not say to you as to Peter: "Do you love Me more than these?" Mother, listen to what He tells you: "*Let* yourself be loved more than these! That is, without fearing that any obstacle will be a hindrance to it, for I am free to pour out My love on whom I wish! '*Let* yourself be loved more than these' is your vocation. It is in being faithful to it that you will make Me happy for you will magnify the power of My love. This love can rebuild what you have destroyed. *Let* yourself be loved more than these."

Dearly loved Mother, if you knew with what assurance I understand God's plan for your soul; it appears to me as in an immense light, and I understand also that in Heaven I will fulfill in my turn a priesthood over your soul. It is Love who associates me with His work in you: Oh, Mother, how great and adorable it is on God's part! And how simple it is for you, and that is exactly what makes it so luminous! Mother, *let* yourself be loved more than the others; that explains everything and prevents the soul from being surprised....

If you will allow her, your little host will spend her Heaven in the depths of your soul: she will keep you in communion with Love, believing in Love; it will be the sign of her dwelling in you. Oh, in what intimacy we are going to live. Cherished Mother, let your life also be spent in the Heavens where I will sing in your name the eternal Sanctus: I will do nothing before the throne of God without you; you know well that I bear your imprint and that something of yourself appeared with your child before the Face of God. I also ask you not to do anything without me; you have granted me this. I will come to live in you. This time I will be your little Mother. I will instruct you, so that my vision will benefit you, that you may participate in it, and that you too, may live the life of the blessed!

Reverend Mother, Mother consecrated for me from eternity, as I leave, I bequeath to you this vocation which was mine in the heart of the Church Militant and which from now on I will unceasingly fulfill in the Church Triumphant: "*The Praise of Glory of the Holy Trinity.*" Mother, "*let* yourself be more loved than these": it is in that way that your Master wills for you to be a praise of glory! He rejoices to build up in you by His love and for His glory, and it is He alone who wants to work in you, even though you will have done nothing to attract this grace except that which a creature can do: works of sin and misery.... He loves you like that. He loves you "more than these." He will do everything in you. He will go to the end: for when a soul is loved by Him to this extent, in this way, loved by an unchanging and creative love, a free love which transforms as it pleases Him, oh, how far this soul will go!

Mother, the fidelity that the Master asks of you is to remain in communion with Love, flow into, be rooted in this Love who wants to mark your soul with the seal of

His power and His love! But in the hours when you feel
only oppression and lassitude, you will please Him even
more if you faithfully *believe* that he is still working, that
He is loving you just the same, and *even more*: because
His love is *free* and that is how He wants to be *magnified*
in you; and you will *let* yourself be loved "*more* than
these." That, I believe, is what this means.... Live in the
depths of your soul! My Master makes me understand
very clearly that He wants to create marvellous things
there: you are called to render homage to the simplicity of
the Divine Being and to magnify the power of His Love.
Believe His "voice" and read these lines as if coming from
him. (LYL 1–6)

"Let yourself be loved." All God wants of us is that we let him love us
and let his love rouse us to love him in return. As Elizabeth was fond
of saying: "It's so simple."

BIBLIOGRAPHY

Balthasar, Hans Urs von. *Two Sisters in the Spirit: Thérèse of Lisieux and Elizabeth of the Trinity*. San Francisco: Ignatius Press, 1992.

Borriello, Luigi. *Spiritual Doctrine of Blessed Elizabeth of the Trinity: Apostolic Contemplative*. Translated by Jordan Aumann. New York: Alba House, 1986.

Benedictines of Stanbrook, eds. *The "Praise of Glory": Reminiscences of Sister Elizabeth of the Trinity, A Carmelite Nun of Dijon (1901–1906)*. New York: Benziger Brothers, 1913.

Carmelite Nuns of Paray-le-Monial. *A Carmelite of the Sacred Heart: The Life of Mère Marie de Jésus, Foundress of the Carmel of Paray-le-Monial (1853–1917)*. Translated by M. E. Arendrup. New York: Benziger Brothers, 1923.

Carmel of Dijon, eds. *Souvenirs*. Paris: Éditions-St. Paul, 1945.

De Meester, Conrad and the Carmel of Dijon, eds. *Light Love Life: A Look at a Face and a Heart*. Translated by Aletheia Kane. Washington, DC: ICS Publications, 1987, 1995, 2012.

Élisabeth de la Trinité. *J'Ai Trouvé Dieu: Oeuvres Complètes* (Tome Ia, Ib, II). Edited by Conrad De Meester. Paris: Éditions du Cerf, 1980, 1980, 1979.

Élisabeth de la Trinité. *Elisabeth de la Trinité: Paroles, annotations personnelles et premiers témoins oculaires* (yet to be published).

Elizabeth of the Trinity. *I Have Found God: The Complete Works* (Vol. One). Edited by Conrad De Meester. Translated by Aletheia Kane. Washington, DC: ICS Publications, 1984, 2014.

Elizabeth of the Trinity. *I Have Found God: The Complete Works* (Vol. Two). Edited by Conrad de Meester. Translated by Anne Englund Nash. Washington, DC: ICS Publications, 1995, 2014.

John of the Cross. *The Spiritual Canticle* in *The Collected Works of St. John of the Cross*. Translated by Kieran Kavanaugh and Otilio Rodriguez. Washingon, DC: ICS Publications, 1991.

Larkin, Thomas. *Elizabeth of the Trinity: Her Life and Spirituality*. Dublin: Carmelite Centre of Spirituality, 1984.

Philipon, M. M. *The Spiritual Doctrine of Elizabeth of the Trinity*. Translated by a Benedictine of Stanbrook Abbey. Washington, DC: Teresian Charism Press, 1985.

Rees, Joan. *Jane Austin: Woman and Writer*. New York: St. Martin Press (London: John Hale & Company), 1976.

Teresa of Avila. *The Way of Perfection* in *The Collected Works of St. Teresa of Avila* (Vol. Two). Translated by Kieran Kavanaugh and Otilio Rodriguez. Washington, DC: ICS Publications, 1980, 2012.

Thérèse of Lisieux. *Story of a Soul: The Autobiography of St. Thérèse of Lisieux*. Translated by John Clarke. Washington, DC: ICS Publications, 1975, 3rd edition 1996.

About Us

ICS Publications, based in Washington, D.C., is the publishing house of the Institute of Carmelite Studies (ICS) and a ministry of the Discalced Carmelite Friars of the Washington Province (U.S.A.) The Institute of Carmelite Studies promotes research and publication in the field of Carmelite spirituality, especially about Carmelite saints and related topics. Its members are friars of the Washington Province.

Discalced Carmelites are a worldwide Roman Catholic religious order comprised of friars, nuns, and laity—men and women who are heirs to the teaching and way of life of Teresa of Avila and John of the Cross, dedicated to contemplation and to ministry in the church and the world.

Information about their way of life is available through local diocesan vocation offices, or from the Discalced Carmelite Friars vocation directors at the following addresses:

Washington Province:
1525 Carmel Road, Hubertus, WI, 53033

California-Arizona Province:
P.O. Box 3420, San Jose, CA 95156

Oklahoma Province:
5151 Marylake Drive, Little Rock, AR 72206

Visit our websites at:
www.icspublications.org and *www.ocdfriarsvocation.org*